Sharing *the* Present

*Mindfulness for Equestrians
& Horse Lovers*

Shreyasi & Frank Brodhecker

Illustrations by Nicole Toren
Photography by Lara Matiisen & Other Photographers

◆ FriesenPress

Suite 300 - 990 Fort St
Victoria, BC, V8V 3K2
Canada

www.friesenpress.com

Copyright © 2021 by Shreyasi and Frank Brodhecker
First Edition — 2021

All rights reserved.

No part of this publication may be reproduced in any form, or by any means, electronic or mechanical, including photocopying, recording, or any information browsing, storage, or retrieval system, without permission in writing from FriesenPress.

Illustrations by Nicole Toren

Photography by Lara Matiisen & Other Photographers

Foreword by Sue McIntosh, MA, CCC

Permission for Select Images from Horses South Australia.
Permission for Dialectical Behavior Therapy Worksheets from The Guilford Press.
Permission for Safety tips from Equine Canada.
Permission for other Photography as credited.

ISBN
978-1-5255-8514-2 (Hardcover)
978-1-5255-8515-9 (Paperback)
978-1-5255-8516-6 (eBook)

1. *Self-Help, Meditations*

Distributed to the trade by The Ingram Book Company

Shreyasi and Frank, Amanda Ubell Photography

Horse-human connection

*The Horse is not here
to reward your ego
to compete with you
to punish you
to control you*

*The Horse responds to
who you are
how you feel
what you think
what you do*

*The Horse is here
to enable you to learn
how to be a better You
—and that is a blessing*

~~ Joanna Verikios

Treasure, Amanda Ubell Photography

TABLE OF CONTENTS

Author Biographies	xi
Dr. Shreyasi Brodhecker MD, FRCP(C) Psychiatry	xi
Frank Brodhecker BSW, RSW (Registered Social Worker)	xvii
Acknowledgements	xix
The expected audience for this book	xx
What is equine-facilitated therapy?	xxi
A note about pronouns	xxii
Foreword: Mindful or mind-full?	xxiii
SECTION 1: Laying the Groundwork	1
Chapter 1: What Is This All About?	3
The horse-human connection – connecting through the senses	5
An evolutionary basis to being in the present moment	6
The value of mindfulness	9
Horse-human interaction: Your attention matters	10
Meaningful conversations with horses happen when we notice our emotions	13
Reading horse body language with mindful awareness	16
Horses feel their own emotions too	20
The benefits of mindfulness for equestrians: a summary	20
Exercises and activities in this book	22
References and resources	26
Chapter 2: Understanding Mindfulness	29
Horses are mindful role models	30
What do I pay attention to?	33
Mindfulness and mindful attitudes	34
Building your mindfulness capacity	50

Research on mindfulness	53
Summary	55
References and resources	56

Chapter 3: Preparing for the Mindfulness Exercises with your Horse ... 61

Taking care of yourself by exploring your Window of Tolerance	62
A conscious shift in routine for you and your horse	69
Taking care of your horse during the exercises	71
Being safe with your horse	71
Noticing general horse body language	80
Horse calming signals	88
Calming a stressed horse	93
Summary	95
References and resources	97

SECTION 2: The Exercises ... 99

Chapter 4: Introducing the Interactive Exercises ... 101

Overview of the exercises	104
Putting it all together	106
Summary	107

Chapter 5: Mindfulness Exercises ... 109

Foundation Exercise: Grounding	109
Exercise #1: Watching—Truly seeing your horse	113
Exercise #2: Breathing and being with your horse	124
Exercise #3: Body awareness near your horse	131
Exercise #4: Touch and connection	139
Exercise #5: Grooming your horse mindfully	147
Exercise #6: Moving with your horse	155
Exercise #7: Riding mindfully—Being one with your horse while riding	168
Exercise #8: Noticing thoughts and emotions—Expectations, judgments, and feelings	176
Exercise #9: Being thankful for your horse	183
Exercise #10: Letting go	189
Exercise #11: Putting it all together	194
Exercise #12: Other ways to be mindful around your horse	198

Summary: Closing reflections ... 203

Shreyasi and Joe, Amanda Ubell Photography

AUTHOR BIOGRAPHIES

Dr. Shreyasi Brodhecker MD, FRCP(C) Psychiatry

What does noticing things happening in the present moment, with non-judgment and kindness, have to do with horses? This book arose from personal and professional influences converging to help me arrive at the answer. The process of noticing in this way is often described as being mindfully aware or "mindful." We all have this gift, and it can be strengthened through practice. Writing this book is an offering to anyone interested in tapping into their innate gifts for wholly inhabiting their experiences in the present moment while in the company of horses.

In my "day job," I work as a psychiatrist. I have an inpatient and community practice that helps seniors suffering from mental illness and/or dementia syndromes. I have a long-standing interest in group psychotherapy and in the application of mindfulness to psychotherapy. In fact, I first learned how mindfulness practices were integrated into psychotherapies during my psychiatric training, when I participated in a Mindfulness-Based Stress Reduction (MBSR) group. Through personal experience I understand how practising mindfulness encourages a deeper self-awareness and offers skills to cope with stress and reduce emotional distress. During my early career, I had the opportunity to co-facilitate MBSR therapy groups and, in 2017-2018, I observed mindfulness-related emotion regulation groups that were based on Dialectical Behavior Therapy (DBT). DBT is explained in some detail in Chapter 2.

Over the years, I have continued to return to these mindfulness practices whenever I feel chaos within myself or my life circumstances. Mindfulness exercises are a way to connect to my authentic self—the part of me that transcends the day-to-day turbulence and allows me to observe the events happening around me with clarity and compassion. When I am with horses, just as with mindfulness, I can connect to my authentic self. This has never been more evident than through this past year with the challenges of the COVID-19 pandemic. My path involves deepening my own practice and embracing the informal mindfulness opportunities that occur when I am spending time among my herd of horses (more about them later), as well as exploring other ways to tune into the present moment, such as journaling and spending time in nature.

How did I find myself on this path? A quote by French philosopher Pierre Teilhard de Chardin helps to explain: "We are not human beings having a spiritual experience; we are spiritual beings having a human experience." Mindfulness practice has helped me attune to a place of calm within myself. At the time of publishing this book, I am opening myself up to a journey of self-compassion, while continuing to strengthen my mindfulness practice.

It is often said that embodied experience in the practice of mindful awareness is a precondition to being able to teach others on this journey. It has become my life's work to share the benefits of being mindfully aware with others around me. I provide seminars on mindfulness and psychotherapy to psychiatry residents at the University of Alberta. My husband Frank and I, along with our colleague Dr. Lori Harper, facilitate short-term emotion regulation groups (with a mindfulness component) for hospitalized older adults dealing with anxiety and depression. Frank and I recently participated in an online MBSR course, and I attended a Mindful Self-Compassion (MSC) group to further deepen my practice. Finally, I am pursuing certification as an MBSR Facilitator with the Centre for Mindfulness Studies in Ontario and hope to train in the future as an MSC Teacher. I facilitate MBSR groups and mindfulness groups for seniors.

I have only recently discovered the world of horses through my husband, Frank. I started riding in 2017, and in the last few years, I began noticing the connection between "horse time" and mindfulness time. Two different events placed me on this path of combining mindfulness with equestrian activities. The first was meeting my "heart horse," Stella. Stella is a seasoned reining horse and a proven broodmare. She is helping me to be a partner with her in the present moment. Thanks to her, I am privileged to be a horse owner, and she introduced me to the healing gift of being with horses. The second event was falling from a much younger and inexperienced horse and breaking my clavicle. That made me realize that horses can be unpredictable and that building a solid horse-human connection helps to reduce the likelihood of such events occurring. I had to slow down after that fracture (my body forced me to), and I began to develop a relationship with my horses that was not based solely on riding. It was during this pause, a place of feeling lost and in limbo because of being unable to ride Stella, that I saw the link between being mindfully aware and achieving true connection with my equine partners.

Anyone who has been around horses can describe feeling unconditionally accepted in their presence (even when there is frustration). Connecting with horses has helped me to heal from my own doubts and insecurities. Part of deepening our mindfulness skills is to be accepting of ourselves. Time spent with horses offers unique opportunities for us to practise these skills in real time. When a person willingly partners with these intelligent creatures, we receive a crash course in living the "full catastrophe," a term borrowed from Jon Kabat Zinn's *Full Catastrophe Living*. Whether I am interacting with horses under saddle or from the ground, partnering with them in therapy, or absorbed in the day-to-day responsibility of managing our equestrian business, I have had to embrace being imperfect; accepting that I do not know all the answers and that routines often have to change. These are situations that foster, and are also enhanced by, mindfulness.

In addition to providing moments to consciously practise mindfulness skills, horse time gives us *natural* moments in which to be mindfully aware with these unique beings. Horses embody a mindful way of experiencing life moments, and we have spontaneous opportunities to be mindfully aware in their presence. This allows us to be better communicators and partners to our horses.

There are days when I feel overwhelmed by various obligations (sometimes those I have set for myself) and there are feelings of unease—feeling like I am out of sync with my values, and less connected to those I care about. These are the days when spending time with our herd helps me to find my way out of this unease and arrive at moments of clarity. Something about being in the presence of a horse shifts me into a mindful state of being, which is the first step to reconnecting to myself and others. No matter how my day goes, being with the horses allows me to rest on the inside, take a deep breath, and fall back into myself, so to speak. I can just be. As I am. They expect nothing else of me.

Then there are the days when, despite feeling clearheaded, I am not able to communicate the right cues to my horse as I practise a riding or groundwork movement or being with them in other ways. I slip into self-critical thoughts, for example that I don't know my horse as well as I thought. I feel anxious or frustrated, and my horse, in turn, becomes confused. This is where mindfulness practice can help both me and my horse. More specifically, if I can take a moment to breathe, actively notice what is happening during these times, recognize this in a kind and patient way, and then shift attention back to my physical movements, I have a better chance of communicating what I want my horse to understand. This may sound strange to some of you, but we hope that you can practise these skills with an open mind to see if they benefit your interactions with your horse.

Learning about horses is a lifelong process. Frank and I have had several skilled coaches and instructors over the years, including Rhonda Bignell of Hawkstone Stables (where we first boarded our horses), Claire Sandercock of Clairety Horsemanship (our current trainer at Spirit Farm Gypsy Cobs Inc.), and Jennifer Maciej of Amethyst Equine Connections (an Equine Facilitated Wellness colleague). We have also been privileged to attend various trainings in Equine Facilitated Wellness in the last year. What we learned at Sue McIntosh's Healing Hooves program in Cremona, Eponaquest©-based workshops with Roxy Wright of Heart's Haven Ranch, and through the Equine Connection™ program near Calgary has echoed what seemed important when first writing this book. *Being* with our horses can be just as impactful—and sometimes more so—than *doing*.

My equestrian goals for the next few years include improving my riding abilities and groundwork skills. I also intend to dually certify as a Mental Health Professional/Learning Professional with Pro EFW (The Professional Association of Equine Facilitated Wellness) in Canada. My dream is to integrate mindfulness practices with helping others to heal around our horses. This dream has manifested into the Mindful Mare Wellness brand, a division of Spirit Farm Gypsy Cobs Inc., which offers individual and group equine facilitated therapy and related virtual courses.

Finally, collaborating with Frank in this project was a practice in humility, patience, and humour. Anyone who knows us can attest that we are caring, but intense people when it comes to our horses. We love them deeply and have committed ourselves to this work. Arriving at common ground during the brainstorming and writing process—in terms of what we wanted to share with readers, figuring out how to describe those ideas while staying true to our individual opinions, and still having fun doing it—was simultaneously energizing and hard work! It was a real privilege, and I look forward to similar collaborations in the future.

Shreyasi

Frank and Joe, Amanda Ubell Photography

Sharing the Present

Frank Brodhecker BSW, RSW (Registered Social Worker)

When I was a 12-year-old child back in Saskatchewan, my parents bought me my first horse—a quarter horse named Tony. I didn't know anything about horses at that time, so I began learning from my uncles and cousins about how to take care of my horse. What I didn't expect was how that horse was going to take care of me.

At that point in my life, I was an overweight child with low self-esteem, and I was doing poorly academically. As I developed a relationship with Tony, I noticed how very comfortable I was in his presence. I felt settled, and I could just be my *real self* around him. I talked to him about the problems I was having—at home and at school. It was the best therapy. Tony listened to me unconditionally, and I could count on him to have his ears pointed attentively towards me, listening. I often cried as I told him things because I was so frustrated, and I always felt better after doing that. As I began to spend more time doing things with Tony, I began to lose weight, and being with him bolstered my self-esteem. I became more confident in myself and I began to try new things, eventually playing soccer and becoming a pitcher for a baseball team. I talked to people more and became more comfortable in my own skin. I began to believe in myself and my capabilities, and I went from a C to an A average in school. When I think back to that time, I realize the talents I developed and the ability to interact with people laid the foundations for my career in social work later in life.

Many years later, as a foster parent, I decided to give each of my foster children their own foal to raise and care for. I knew that as the foal grew, it would, in turn, "take care" of the child. I witnessed this amazing transformation firsthand with my three-year-old foster son, who came to my home functionally limited, but flourished in the company of the twelve horses we owned. He too, grew to achieve both academically and athletically in his teens.

At the age of 30, I decided I no longer wanted to work in industrial sales, and I went back to school. I remembered my days with Tony, and how I had enjoyed becoming more socially outgoing. I decided on a career in social work. The competition was stiff (only 85/475 applicants were being accepted), but I made it! The first week in class, I knew it was the right place for me. After obtaining my Bachelor of Social Work degree from the University of Calgary, I started working as a registered social worker in seniors' mental health at Alberta Hospital Edmonton. I've now been working in this field for over 15 years.

I've always been especially interested in observing horse behaviours and developing relationships with these animals, particularly with young foals, whose trust I had to gain. I sometimes sat outside watching my herd in -25 degrees Celsius, waiting for one of my foals to become comfortable enough to walk up to me. In addition to raising foals, my horse experience extends to halter breaking foals, starting young horses (both from the ground and under saddle), horse husbandry, and showing our Gypsy Cob horses. In the summer of 2019, before life in the pandemic, I showed some of our Gypsy Cob horses at the Alberta Feathered Horse Classic in Red Deer, which I intend to do again as soon as I am able. Shreyasi and I continue to receive instruction from other experienced equestrian mentors. Being with horses means life-long learning, to which we are both committed. I also enjoy trail riding with my retired reiner, Romeo.

Shreyasi introduced me to mindfulness practices and some of the more popular mindfulness-based literature, while I, in turn, introduced Shreyasi to horses. As I began learning about mindfulness, she began learning about horses. We now have a herd of 15 horses, and it continues to grow.

In 2017 and 2018, I observed an advanced skills groups based on dialectical behavior therapy, along with Shreyasi and our colleague Dr. Harper. After modifying the content into a group therapy curriculum for seniors with anxiety and depression, we began facilitating an "emotion regulation group." From there, we realized that mindfulness and horses could complement each other, and that sparked the idea for this book.

I recently participated in an MBSR group through the Centre for Mindfulness Studies in Ontario. We now run equine facilitated therapy programs to help people who are struggling with their emotions—offering them tools and experiences to cope with the day-to-day challenges that life brings with it. I have thoroughly enjoyed exploring the link between partnering with horses and giving clients the chance to form healthy attachments, and I am currently working towards my dual certification as a mental health professional and learning professional with Pro-EFW. We look forward to sharing our horses' healing with others in our Mindful Mare Wellness program.

I sincerely hope that this book is helpful and will add a therapeutic dimension to your life, as it has to ours.

Frank

Sharing the Present

Acknowledgements

We would like to acknowledge the following individuals who generously contributed their time, experience, and wisdom towards the development of this book. We thank Sue McIntosh of Healing Hooves Equine Facilitated Wellness Program, Cremona, Alberta and Rhonda and Sheldon Bignell of Hawkstone Stables, Spruce Grove, Alberta. We would like to especially thank Donna-Lee Wybert of TextualMatters for her insight and masterful editing of our manuscript. We further thank Sushmitha Gollapudi, Natalie Wilson, Dr. Lori Harper, and Dr. Kate Hibbard for their edits of select sections of the manuscript.

We celebrate Nicole Toren of Handgallop Studio and Tonic Equestrian for her creative genius and illustrations. We extend gratitude to Nancy Christy-Moore of Nancy Christy-Moore Art for her permission to reproduce *Salt River Run*, a painting that holds a special place in our hearts and home, as the book's cover design. We are grateful to have received copyright permission from Equestrian Canada, Horse South Australia, and the Guilford Press for select material in the book.

Lara Matiisen of Next to Wild Photography generously offered us her expertise and vision for photographic images used in this book. Photographs of us and the Spirit Farm Gypsy Cobs Inc. herd have also been provided by the following equine photographers: Trisia Eddy of Prairie Darkroom Photography, Amanda Ubell of Amanda Ubell Photography, and Samantha Callioux of SJ Originals Photography. We would like to thank ALL our friends in the equestrian community who generously provided photographs of their personal time with their horses for specific mindfulness exercises in the book. These friends include Stephanie Dewes of Miracle Mile Equine Center, Desiree Sieben of Mane Equestrian Athletics, Jennifer Maciej of Amethyst Equine Connections, and Katie Hembree of KD Performance Horses.

We would also like to thank our friends and family who have helped us through this process. We have a team of dedicated and inspiring staff who help us to make this dream happen though consistent hard work. We especially thank our son and Farm Manager, Erich Brodhecker, who assists us through the ups and downs of life at a farm with equanimity and competence. Watching our grandson Braxton with Erich and spending time with the herd at Spirit Farm Gypsy Cobs Inc. reminds us of the importance of *being* and not *doing* all the time. Thank you both for these moments.

Finally, this book would not have been possible without the interactions and opportunities for daily mindfulness from our horses, past and present: Stella, Romeo, Joe, Gucci, Espresso, Sid, Violet, Jazz, Grace, Rhianna, Sammy, Anise, Arya, Honey, Lucky, Fiona, Treasure, Tony, and many others. *We love you all!*

Erich and Joe,
Amanda Ubell Photography

The expected audience for this book

The exercises in this book are intended to help readers from a variety of backgrounds to discover alternative ways of being with their horses and to complement their current understanding of horses. We invite both beginner and experienced equestrians to engage in these exercises. We hope that you can use them to deepen your connection with your horse and to develop your observational abilities.

We also hope that this book will be a resource for people who are interested in simply being around horses and experiencing a connection with these incredible beings. We acknowledge that various readers have differing levels of skill, training, and credentials. You don't have to ride horses to benefit from and carry out most of the exercises in this book.

If you have an interest in mindfulness and the ability to be near horses, you can practise these exercises. Although there are several discussions about horses specifically, the mindfulness concepts described may also overlap with yoga, meditation, or other practices you have tried before.

If you are a qualified equine therapy practitioner and this material falls within your equine and human services scope of practice, these exercises may be useful within your specific program or with certain clients, especially those with an interest or background in mindfulness practices. We appreciate that practitioners may bring various levels of experience in working with people who struggle with mental health difficulties. Regardless of your prior experience, we trust that these exercises will be helpful, whether personally or professionally.

Since our intended audience will likely have different learning styles and preferences, we offer you access to audio guided exercises and videos at our website, www.mindfulmarewellness.com, to complement the printed text in this book.

What is equine-facilitated therapy?

While we expect that some readers may be familiar with this term, we hope that other readers will find it helpful to understand who these professionals are and the types of therapies they engage in. In particular, equine-facilitated therapy explores the role of horses in supporting human healing, which may include both physical and psychological wellness. Many models incorporate mindfulness principles into their approaches. There exists a diverse community of practitioners that includes, but is not limited to, the following activities:

- Equine-Facilitated Wellness (EFW)
- Equine-Facilitated Counselling (EFC)
- Equine-Facilitated Mental Health (EFMH)
- Equine-Assisted Learning (EAL)
- Animal-Assisted Therapy (AAT)
- Therapeutic riding

Considering these many approaches, our vision is that interested equine-facilitated therapy practitioners may find these exercises useful, while remaining within the boundaries of their existing scopes of practice.

A note about pronouns

In much of this book we have kept with the growing trend to use they/them/their as gender-neutral singular pronouns. This makes for simpler writing, but your equine partners may include colts, fillies, geldings, stallions, and mares. We hope that these pronouns make for inclusive and easy reading that provides you with the space to imagine your own horse.

FOREWORD
Mindful or mind-full?

by Sue McIntosh

There are so many things for us to fill our minds with nowadays: the endless list of things we need to get done before we pick up the kids; whether we'll get that job we applied for; what our friend *really* meant in that text she sent the other day. At the same time, we are surrounded by a myriad of options for distracting ourselves from anything that may feel too vulnerable—like our emotions or an awareness of ourselves. Whether our distraction is online shopping, social media, or even working, it is all too easy to avoid spending any quiet time with ourselves. Busy becomes our mantra, our expectation for ourselves and others, our badge of pride.

Yet both brain research and common sense tell us that, just as a child grows physically during sleep when her body is at rest, for us to grow and heal emotionally, we need emotional rest. *Mind-full* is emotional work. *Mindful* is emotional rest.

I doubt any of this is news to you. Mindfulness has become a buzzword we hear regularly, something most of us know we should do more of, be better at. But *how?*

My personal journey with mindfulness has not been smooth. I've struggled with being mind-full much of my life, and while I've tried things like yoga and meditation intermittently, I am the person who is falling out of poses at the back of the class. There is a very noisy monkey in my head who perks up the moment I even contemplate meditation.

Yet I have come to recognize that I can, and do, experience emotional rest in my life and often right in the midst of life's ups and downs; I just find that

I rest with animals—and particularly with horses. It's with them that my mind gets less busy, and I start to notice and appreciate what is happening, or not happening, right in the moment—just the way it is. As I move into "horse time," I become more aware of what I feel in my body, I tune into all five of my senses, and I start to breathe. I move from *mind-full* to *mindful*.

My desire to share this healing with others was an impetus for my career change 25 years ago, and led to the formation of Healing Hooves, a counselling and professional training program in equine and animal-assisted therapy. A key goal of our sessions at Healing Hooves is to slow down, to make space, and to be in the moment. This is where I find healing and growth start to happen, and it is the presence and nature of horses that creates an environment that invites this.

So, when Frank and Shreyasi told me about their plans for this book and asked for my support and input, everything within me cried out, *yes!*

The world needs this book.

People like me need this book.

I believe our horses want us to read this book.

Working with Frank and Shreyasi has been both a joy and a privilege. They are both highly credentialled and qualified professionals, and yet they have a willingness to collaborate with other professionals, seeking feedback and considering other's perspectives, which is refreshing and inspiring. This book reflects their diligence to research, and their openness to considering perspectives from a wide range of mental health and equine professionals.

Their understanding and respect for horses as sentient beings, with the ability to experience and the right to express their own emotions, shines through. Consideration for the horse's experience is paramount in every exercise, resulting in exercises that are not just good for you; they will hopefully be a great experience for your horse too! Throughout these activities, Frank and Shreyasi have also paid close attention—recognizing that horses are not people. They realize that working with them means we need to honour and respect this fact to keep everyone safe.

Something else you will find in this book is an invitation to incorporate and understand mindfulness with horses in a way that fits you, your life, and your way of understanding and relating to horses, yourself, and the world.

Sharing the Present

Frank and Shreyasi are not telling you what to believe and they are not trying to make you see everything as they do. Nevertheless, they encourage you to reflect and challenge yourself as you go through a process, to allow yourself to make mistakes and to change your mind. We are all students in this world, and this book provides empathic encouragement and support, rather than restrictive rules.

I first met Frank and Shreyasi a couple of years ago on a sunny afternoon at Healing Hooves. We spent a mindful afternoon with the horses, and I was struck by the sense of grounded-ness that seemed to be a part of their very beings. They were seeking guidance from *me* about equine therapy, and yet I felt emotionally richer and fulfilled from my time with *them* that day. The world needs this book, and Frank and Shreyasi are uniquely and wonderfully equipped to create it.

I hope you enjoy it as much as I did.

Sue McIntosh MA, CCC, Healing Hooves Equine Facilitated Wellness
April 16, 2019.

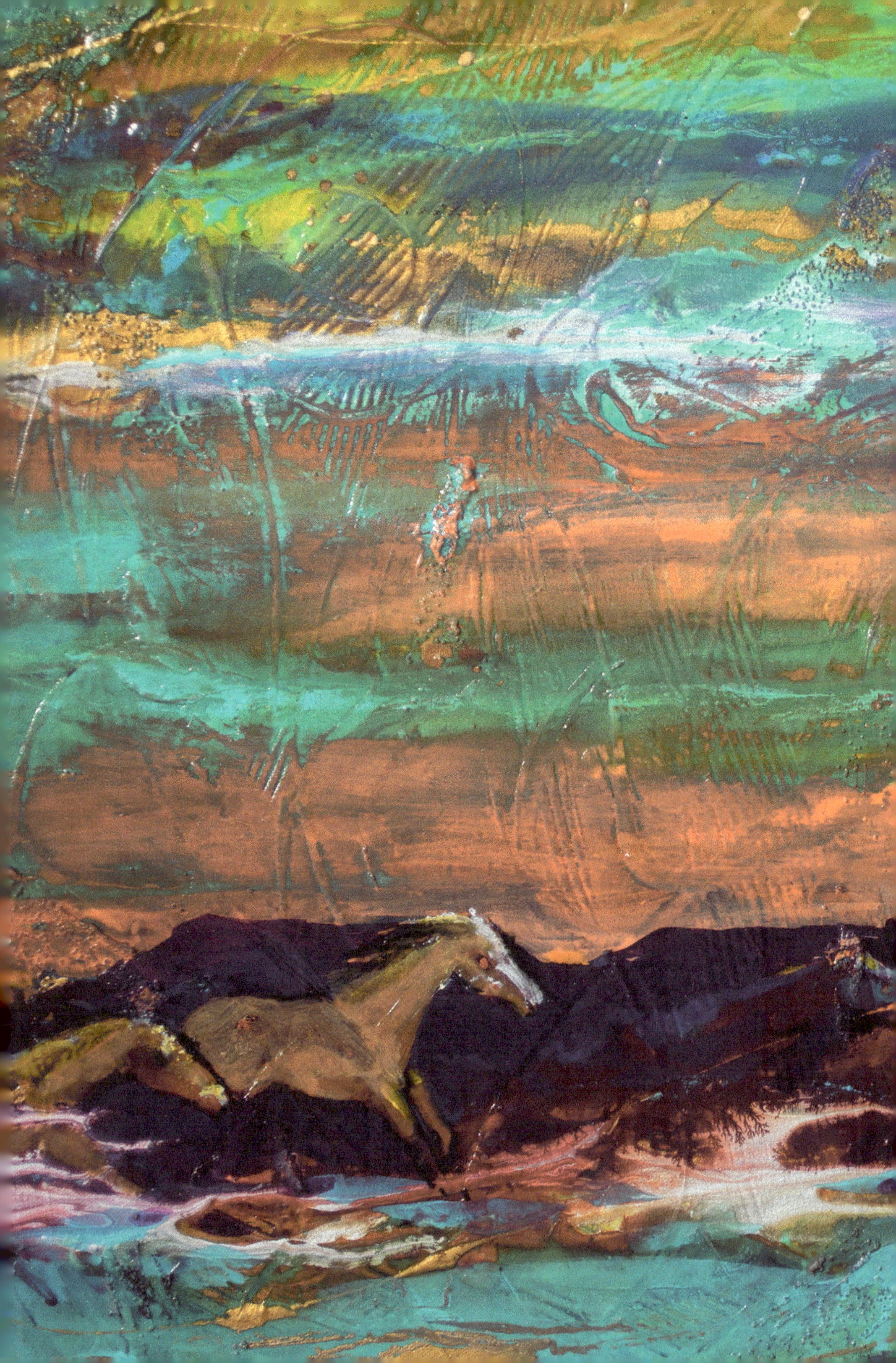

SECTION 1
Laying the Groundwork

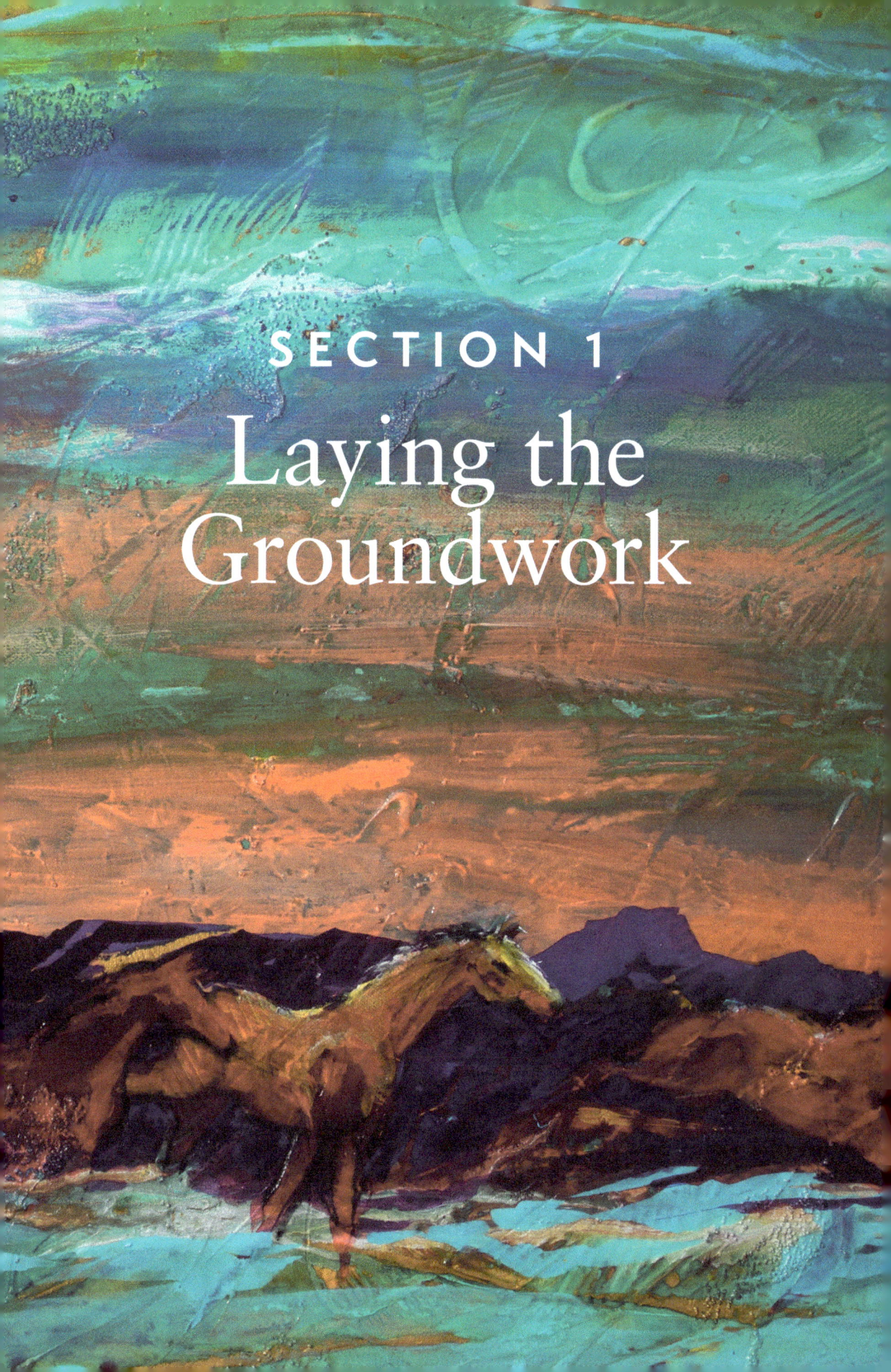

Shreyasi and Frank Brodhecker

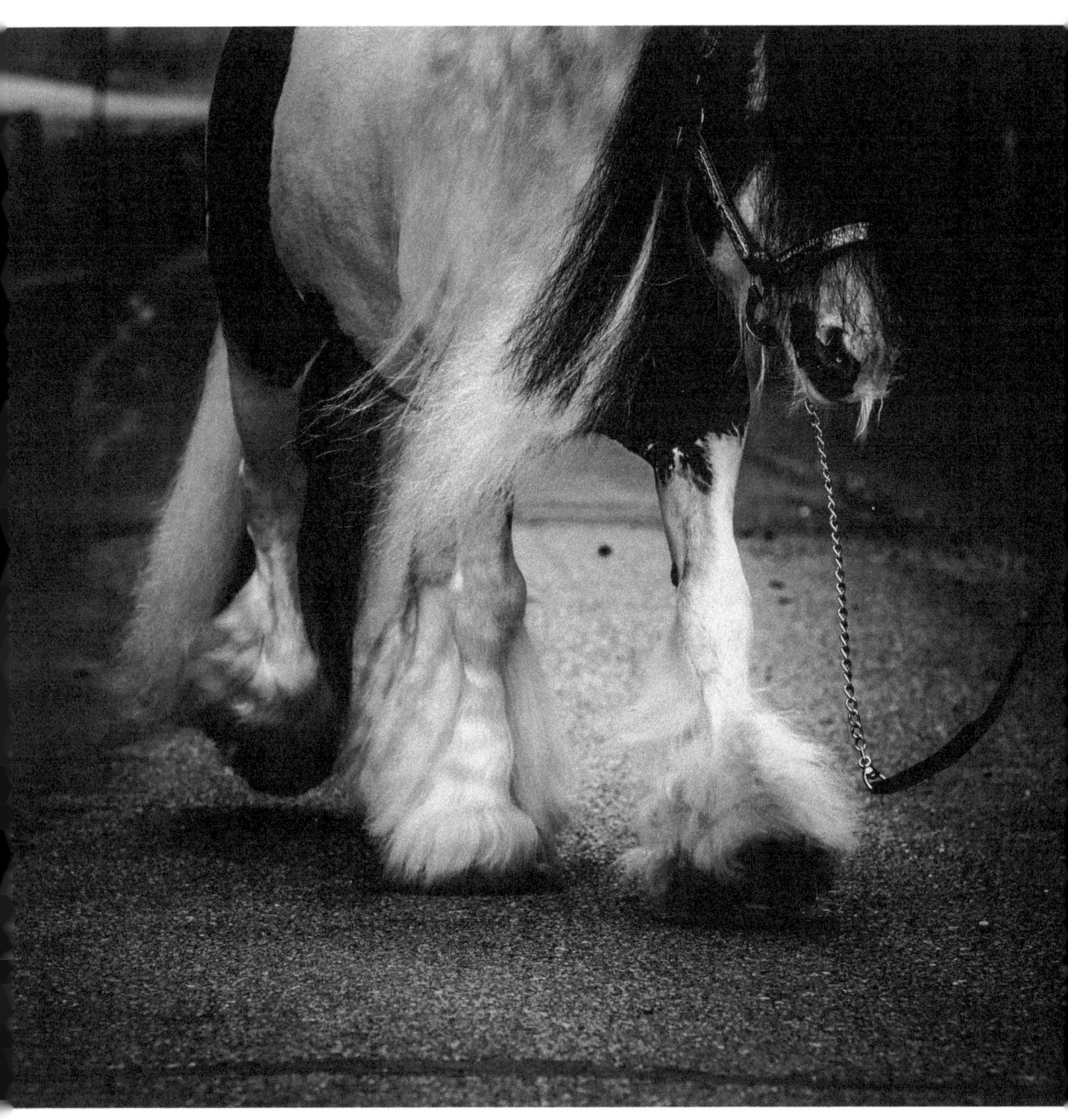

Joe, SJ Originals Photography

CHAPTER 1

What Is This All About?

This project evolved by merging our love of horses with our journey in mindfulness to create a different way of connecting with our equine partners. Sometimes, various paths integrate harmoniously at the right time. This book came into being once we realized that two apparently unrelated pursuits, the time we spend with our horses and our personal mindfulness practices, are, at their core, both ways to access being in the present moment.

Being mindful refers to being fully aware of events in the present moment while staying curious and accepting of whatever arises. Anyone exploring practices in mindfulness is familiar with the emphasis on real-life experience helping to understand what being mindful is about. Another way of putting this is learning from the inside out. There is a balance between didactic and experiential learning when exploring the concepts of mindful awareness. We have attempted to strike this balance without the benefits of learning together in person through offering a brief section of background theory in Chapter 2 and practice via the mindful exercises and post-exercise reflections, which form the heart of the book. The mindful exercises are uniquely geared to time spent with horses.

We noticed something interesting as we spent time with our horses and gathered an expanding knowledge of handling and riding skills from our coaches and trainers; the unique attention skills that equestrians employ, when caring for and training their horses, *overlapped* with the mindfulness skills that we were practising and teaching others. We found that when we intentionally paid attention, in a certain way, to what was happening during sessions—which is how you invite mindful awareness—the connection to our horses felt natural and close. As we watched and handled our yearlings, we were also reminded of the importance of being present to what our horses are doing in each moment both for safety and building trust. Such present awareness, characterized by openness to whatever arises, is what mindfulness is all about.

This link between horse time and practising mindfulness skills can arise in different ways. When we pay attention in a certain way, we notice more and respond intentionally, becoming better communicators with our horses. Horses are also experts at being mindfully aware, and they naturally focus awareness on the present moment. Being around them invites us into the same state of being, and we can explore paying attention to each present moment that we spend with them. Horses model several of the mindful attitudes, which are described in more detail in Chapter 2.

There are numerous books available on developing equestrian skills and creating a harmonious working relationship with your horse. In our experience, the elements that create a harmonious connection with our horses are the same ones that create mindful relationships with ourselves and others. In this book, we synthesize two parallel streams of knowledge—relationship-based equestrian approaches and mindfulness practice—into a simple way of being *present* with horses that anyone can practise. Some of the ideas explored in this work are loosely drawn from the concepts of Centered Riding® as described by Sally Swift, Connected Riding® by Peggy Cummings, Tellington *TTouch*® by Linda Tellington-Jones, and from our interpretation and understanding of the teachings from various instructors, including Rhonda Bignell, Claire Sandercock, and Jennifer Maciej.

On our journey this past year, we have been fortunate to connect with like-minded individuals who have a growing recognition of the benefits of mind-body practices for equestrian personal development. They acknowledge the relationship between these practices and building physical flexibility. The impact of thought patterns and physical tension on attaining personal goals is also recognized. We would like to acknowledge equine-facilitated wellness professionals Sue McIntosh and Roxy Wright for the learnings that further reinforced the ideas and practices in this book.

Thus, several sources have contributed to our knowledge and shaped the writing of this book—equestrian, professional, personal, and spiritual. We have amalgamated these diverse sources and blended them with our own ideas, yielding an original, creative, and practical approach that has helped us improve as horse people. The synthesis of these influences is ours. When individuals have provided unique material, however, we have quoted these contributions in the text.

This book is not about *doing things* with horses; it is about *being* with horses and creating a foundation for other training to further strengthen the horse-human partnership. It is about helping you tune in to the present moment with your horse, which we hope can create a deeper connection with these majestic beings, regardless of experience level.

> *Horses have an emotional impact on the people near them. If you have previously been around horses, reflect on some moments when this has held true for you.*

The horse-human connection – connecting through the senses

There is a sense of joy—easy to experience, but hard to describe—that characterizes how it feels to be around horses. Horses seem to have a positive impact on people's energy. An often-cited example of the tangible, calming effects that horses have on humans' autonomic nervous systems when they spend time together is the 2013 research completed by Dr. Gehrke, in collaboration with the HeartMath Institute.

The Gehrke study suggests that the well-being many people experience when they are near horses is related to the horses' calming effects on human physiological states. Notably, as a horse's heart is anatomically approximately five times larger than that of a human, some people believe that the larger electromagnetic field around the heart is associated with the horse's calming impact on humans. This interaction appears to be reciprocal, and humans can influence their horses with the quality and intensity of their non-verbal cues. Some refer to this as your "energy." We discuss how to become more aware of your energy and how to use it intentionally to achieve a meaningful connection with your horse, later in the book.

An evolutionary basis to being in the present moment

As well as the potential to calm the human body, horses offer people the amazing gift of fully living in the here and now. Horses are continuously paying attention to the present. It is their innate way of being. They are completely tuned in to what their sight, sound, touch, taste, and smell detect in each moment. Another way to understand this is recognizing that horses are instinctively mindful. Horses can *sustain* attention in the present moment while focusing on various things at once; they also *divide* their attention between their surroundings, their herd, and the humans they are interacting with.

Attentive horse

Focusing awareness entirely on the present has evolutionary advantages for the herd. Pat Parelli, a natural horsemanship trainer says, "When something startles the herd, there is no time to communicate the need to flee by anything other than the reactive nervous system" (McFarland, Parelli & Parelli, 2011). Being sophisticated prey animals, horses operate by relying on sensory information. Their processing has been described as intuitive, instinctual, and sensory based; thus, they are highly attuned to others in their herd, which better ensures their survival. Horses have the ability to detect human emotions just as they pick up on other stimuli in their environment. Regardless of whether people are seen as fellow members of the herd or as a potential threat, it is evolutionarily advantageous for horses to detect what humans nearby are feeling, emotionally and physically, from one moment to the next.

Herd in motion

Attentive herd, SJ Originals Photography

Herd in motion, Prairie Darkroom Photography

Simply being around horses allows you to experience present moment awareness. Partnering with your horse in this way helps you to establish a connection because you can have a first-hand view of their ways of experiencing the world. We hope that practising the mindfulness exercises as outlined in this book will help you tune into these moments more often throughout the day, in this way practising outside of your time with horses. These exercises will also help to strengthen your capacity to be present more of the time in your relationships with yourself, with others, and in nature.

The value of mindfulness

"Mindfulness" or "mindful awareness" refers to noticing things exactly as they are happening right now—with intention and willingness to accept whatever is seen or felt. In the words of Dr. Shapiro and Dr. Carlson in their book, *The Art and Science of Mindfulness*, mindful awareness is about "intentionally attending to the present in an open, caring, and discerning way" (Shapiro and Carlson, 2009). Although everyone has had moments of "living in the present", practising such skills on a regular basis can help you to spend more time in that state of being. People differ in the extent to which they are innately mindful, but regular practice can further grow that natural capacity. Mindfulness skills require lifelong practice, and we also continue to build our skills every day.

> *What does it mean to be present with your horse? With yourself? With someone else? Can you tell the difference between being distracted and being fully attentive during interactions with others?*

Research has shown that regularly practising mindfulness with intention can improve a variety of cognitive skills such as attention, working memory, and the ability to regulate emotions, so that you can cope better with various stressors. Mindfulness practice can reduce caregiver burnout and has been integrated into therapies for treating depression, anxiety, and self-destructive behaviours. It has also been associated with the reduction of chronic pain, improvement of self-compassion, and a greater period of time experiencing positive, rather than negative, emotions. You will find a list of mindfulness resources and research articles at the end of Chapter 2.

Horse-human interaction: Your attention matters

For equestrians, acquiring the basics of groundwork (working your horse from the ground when you are standing or moving with your horse) and riding usually involve improving body awareness and position. This requires remaining focused on the task at hand and communicating clearly with your horse, so they learn and remember what you are asking of them when you apply certain cues. When your body is tense, or is not aligned with the horse's movement, it is harder to adjust and to stay flexible from one moment to the next. At times like this, the cues you give your horse may not match what you intended. Just as your body can play a huge role in how smoothly your work with your horse goes, so can the state of your mind. When you are distracted, your horse senses this, and as a result, your time together does not flow smoothly.

Clearly, the quality of your attention affects the time you spend with your horse, but it is helpful to remember that your *emotional* state also makes a big impact—and horses are keenly aware of your emotions. Although they cannot label your emotions, their sensory capacities allow them to detect shifts in your body occurring when you feel certain emotions.

Increasingly, scientists are beginning to appreciate what most horse people have known for years: horses are sentient beings with the ability to communicate a range of emotions and detect emotions in the humans around them (Smith et al., 2016).

Sentience has been defined in various ways, including the ability to perceive and feel emotions, the ability to be aware of one's surroundings, and the ability to choose one's actions. We base our definition of sentience on "The Cambridge Declaration on Consciousness" (Low, 2012). A consensus reached by a varied group of neuroscientists in July 2012 declared that animals with sentience possess "conscious states along with the capacity to exhibit intentional behaviors" (Low, 2012).

Sharing the Present

When horses detect your emotional state, they can reflect this back to you in comparable, emotionally intense ways. So, if you are distracted or upset around your horse, your horse may respond by becoming uneasy or confused. On the other hand, your calm energy sends the message to your horse that everything is safe right now. This allows your horse, being a prey animal for whom safety is the main priority, to reflect calm energy in turn.

Similarly, horses can generate their own emotional states, which are dependent on the situation they are in. There can be many reasons why your horse may feel anxious or stressed. Just as with people, certain horses are more sensitive in detecting and reacting to the emotional state of the people around them. Our intention here is *not* for you to start judging yourself if your horse is behaving from a place of anxiety or frustration. Rather, we encourage you to notice that you can often influence whether your horse is calmer or more anxious.

We realize that people may conceptualize the interactions between horses and humans in different ways. Some may not agree that horses can discern human energy and instead prefer to view horses as sensitive prey animals that are biologically attuned to the non-verbal signals of the people and animals around them. Others are comfortable with the notion that horses perceive energy in themselves, other animals, and people. Both perspectives derive from the premise that horses detect and respond to shifts inside us. To better understand the ideas we share in this book about the dialogue between horses and humans, we invite you to openly consider the possibility that horses detect and respond to humans' subtle nonverbal messages. Think of this by using a term of your choosing like "energy," "nonverbal body language," or "nonverbal states" to facilitate understanding.

Shreyasi and Frank Brodhecker

Soulful Joe, Prairie Darkroom Photography

Meaningful conversations with horses happen when we notice our emotions

This section expands on the idea that we affect our horses emotionally, and vice versa. We hope to spark your curiosity, not your self-judgment, about the effect you have on your horses, and to encourage you to start noticing what is happening for you if they seem restless or uneasy. Please remember that self-criticism does not serve you or your horse. Rather than attacking yourself for what you may be doing wrong, "it's about shifting focus" (McIntosh, 2019). In the words of the spiritual writer Rick Warren, "Humility is not thinking less of ourselves, it is thinking of ourselves less" (Warren, 2012). This is the approach we have found most helpful when working in the world of horses, where each day reminds us of how much more there is to learn about these complex and fascinating creatures.

Given this complexity, your ability to mindfully notice what you are feeling and what the horses around you may be feeling, can powerfully shape the time you spend with them. If you are experiencing certain emotions without realizing it, it will be difficult to forge a connection with your horse—and the likelihood of a successful session is diminished. For example, if you are tired and frustrated after a long workday, you may filter out important information about the surroundings, your horse's body language, and even how your own body physically feels. When you are frustrated or anxious, even if you pretend you are fine, your horse notices this incongruence and may therefore perceive potential "dangers" in the environment. They, in turn, may become distracted and nervous.

Such emotions may arise during a session, and your horse may respond to them, even when you have no clue about what you are really feeling. Or your horse may also be stressed for reasons completely unrelated to you, and if you are "caught up" in your own emotions, it will prevent you from noticing and responding clearly to the situation in front of you. In any of these scenarios, neither you nor your horse can truly settle into the session and fully pay attention to what you are doing together.

Conversely, when you *notice* emotions appearing, it adds clarity to your experience. You feel connected to what is happening *right now*. This knowledge allows you to feel less overwhelmed, and your horse responds to your balanced energy (which can also be thought of as your "body language" or "state of being"). Things flow more smoothly, movements are confident and fluid, and the session feels more natural, regardless of what you hope to achieve during that time. It's okay to be sad, scared, or frustrated as long as you *realize* this. If you feel overwhelmed by your emotions, you can either decide not to work with your horse that day, or you can proceed—*while staying aware of those emotions and the impact on your horse during the session.*

So, how do you develop the ability to become more aware of your feelings and those of your horse? Through mindfulness practice. Taking a few moments to simply notice your breathing, before you go out to meet your horse, is one way to reach this place of clear observation. This helps you to release intense emotions or challenging thoughts from your day. It also helps you to avoid planning ahead, and instead become fully involved in what is happening *right now* with your horse. We describe this more during the mindfulness exercises later in the book.

Intense feelings or troubling thoughts can surface *during* your horse time. This might be related to something that is happening in the session or something completely unrelated. These thoughts and feelings tend to absorb your focus and shift your attention away from the rest of your *present moment* experience. Taking a few deep breaths or noticing your breathing without changing it can help at these times, too. Although the feelings and thoughts may remain, they will no longer be the primary focus of your attention. Try this when you notice emotional discomfort or physical tension during a session with your horse. In Chapter 3, we offer examples of how you can release such tension before and during time spent with your horse. The first exercise in Section 2 also provides an activity to calm your energy before meeting your horse.

> *Do you agree or disagree with the advice of leaving your problems at the barn door before spending time with your horse?*

There are other ways to respond mindfully when you are distracted by feelings or thoughts during horse time. Besides taking a few deep breaths or noticing your natural breathing rate, you can focus on your five senses. This is described in detail in Chapter 3. For example, notice what you see around you, what you hear, what you smell, taste, or touch with your hands in that moment. Sue McIntosh of Healing Hooves Animal Assisted Therapy describes this as "noticing the air as you breathe and the ground under your feet as anchors to feel safe and grounded in the present moment" (S. McIntosh, personal communication, January 10, 2019).

Another way to deal with emotions and thoughts surfacing during horse time is to imagine a container, in whatever form you like. Imagine temporarily placing the intense feelings and thoughts in this container when they arise. You can open the container later when you choose. The container metaphor is well known in various types of psychotherapy, and it "cannot be a delete button" (S. McIntosh, personal communication, February 14, 2019) where you shut everything off permanently. Rather, you are invited to think of this visual metaphor as pressing a pause button so that you can reflect on these feelings and thoughts later.

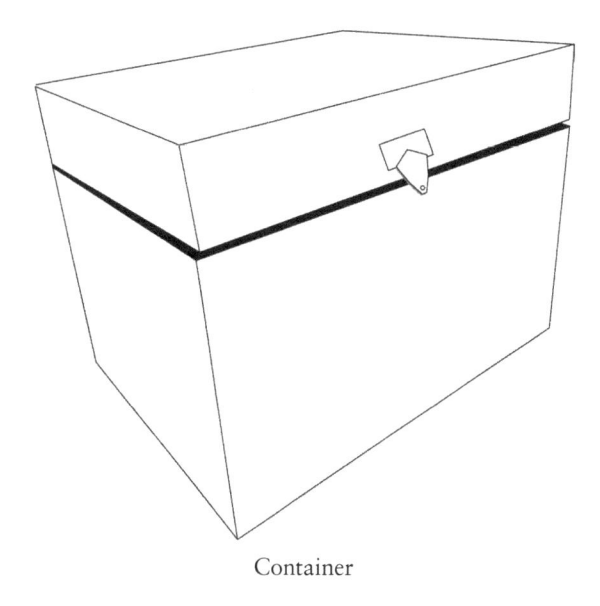

Container

Please note that none of the exercises in this book are meant to replace counselling and/or therapy. If you'd like to explore these thoughts and feelings in depth, we suggest that you find another place to do this, with those you trust, or with a mental health professional. It is safer, for you and your horse, if in-depth exploration occurs when you are not engaging in these exercises with your horse.

If you are dealing with severe emotional distress or mental health issues when reading this book, we urge you to complete the exercises with a certified equine-facilitated wellness (EFW) mental health professional. This will ensure that a qualified professional is available to debrief you about your experiences and provide support during the exercises, as needed. Such professionals have the training and experience to see and respond to the needs of both the horse and human clients. If you wish to learn more about what an EFW professional does, how to become certified as an EFW professional, or to obtain a list of Canadian certified EFW professionals, please visit www.equinefacilitatedwellness.org.

As you may have already noticed, we use the terms "feelings" and "emotions" interchangeably in this book. We recognize that readers with a mental health background likely make a distinction between the two. Such discussion is outside the scope of this book, and as such, we use these terms interchangeably to refer to what you experience when you consciously feel sadness, shame, guilt, frustration, and so forth.

Reading horse body language with mindful awareness

Since horses live in the present, your connection with them deepens when you reciprocate this focus. You start taking note of things you may have previously overlooked. For instance, you may observe how your horse's gaze shifts when looking across the horizon, scanning specific sights and listening to sounds. You may discern the position of the horse's ears and neck, their general stance, and other nonverbal communication signals. It is helpful to recall that horses initially display subtle cues that intensify into stronger behaviours if they are unable to get their message across. For example, a horse that has pinned their ears back and is using their body to assert their physical space is sending the message to herd members that they expect them to move out of their space. This horse will progress to kicking or biting if their initial signals are ignored by the herd members.

When you can mindfully detect your horse's subtle messages early in a conversation by being "in the moment," it gives you the opportunity to respond intentionally. This may reduce the likelihood of escalated behaviours related to fear, confusion, or aggression and may also quicken your responses at these times. We expand on this topic more in Chapter 2 with an example of working with one of our previous horses, Arya. When we talk about paying attention

Sharing the Present

to the conversation with your horse with openness and curiosity, we mean paying attention with *your eyes and your body*—in other words, observing what you see in your environment and what you feel inside your body. These attention skills can be strengthened by regular mindfulness practice.

Standing horse

Lucky and Treasure (Lucky in foreground), SJ Originals Photography

Having meaningful conversations with your horse is vital to success in the horse-human relationship. Regardless of where you and your horse end up on your shared journey, mindful communication allows for better conversations. To participate fully during your sessions—whether you have specific goals or are just spending time together—be aware of your body's internal sensations, thoughts, and movements, along with reading your horse's specific cues. As you become familiar with this process and become more attuned, you may notice that a certain ear position, look, tilt of the head and neck, or swishing tail predicts a specific behavioural outcome. Alternately, picking up on particular body sensations or feelings may alert you to certain responses in your horse.

When you can read these non-verbal cues in your horse, you can adjust your behaviour to communicate clearly what you want them to do next. Doing this will improve and enrich the quality of the non-verbal conversation between you both and demonstrate to your horse that you are observant, responsive, and able to act with fair leadership.

When watching equestrians who are attuned to their horses, you may see how closely they pay attention. One of our previous trainers emphasized that: "Experienced equestrians easily stay in the present moment since this aligns with the horse's need" (R. Bignell, personal communication, March 21, 2019). This is why mindfulness exercises are such a good fit for your relationship with your horse. Being able to focus with intention is also an asset when performing under the highly stressful conditions of showing and competing.

> *Mindful awareness is about noticing the present moment, while letting it be the way it is. Your senses can "anchor" you in the present moment.*

A horse's behaviour can change from session to session, and no two horses are completely alike. This requires flexibility on your part; the more you practise these mindfulness exercises, the easier it will become for you to flexibly attune to the present. This is like brain training to make you a better horse person. If you apply these skills to other parts of your daily experiences, you may notice that you make decisions or solve problems more effectively, in general.

> *Have you had times when being aware of the present moment helped you to adjust to your horse's behaviours?*

Horses feel their own emotions too

Sometimes, people tune out their emotions and ignore the effect they have on the horses with whom they spend time. Other times, people closely read their horse's body language, but forget that horses have emotions of their own. As we have already said, horses might have reasons other than your presence to be excited or stressed, or to otherwise react emotionally around you. You cannot assume that your horse's emotions are **always** because of you; nor can you assume that you have **zero** impact on your horse's emotional state. The truth lies somewhere in between. Within this frame of reference, your emotions and those of your horse can be witnessed **as they actually are** at any specific moment in a session.

> *Remember that you have an emotional impact on your horse, but they are also capable of having feelings that have nothing to do with you.*

The benefits of mindfulness for equestrians: a summary

Many in the equestrian world recognize that an equestrian's physical imbalances contribute to their horse's physical limitations or challenges. This makes intuitive sense because a physiological kinship develops between a horse and their rider. When a rider achieves physical balance in their seat and their movements, their horse has a far greater likelihood of optimal function and balance. The consequences of not attaining such physical balance are evident during riding and when horses require physical therapies such as chiropractic and massage.

Sharing the Present

The Centered Riding® and Connected Riding® approaches that we mentioned previously describe exercises for riders to maintain and improve balance and strength when on their horses. While these equestrian approaches may not explicitly describe mindfulness, their concepts are remarkably parallel. Just as in specific mindfulness practices, these exercises emphasize paying attention to your bodily sensations in the present moment and intentionally shifting them, if you choose.

From our perspective, equestrians' emotional balance further contributes to enhancing their horse's wellness and their capacity to achieve their full potential. Emotional balance is a term we use to describe when you are able to notice how you are feeling and not be overwhelmed by those feelings. Building mindfulness skills will help you stay aware and be less overwhelmed by your emotions over time, and it also teaches you to be kinder to yourself and accept whatever arises for you from one moment to the next. This kind, accepting stance eventually extends naturally to your approach to your horse. As a summary, some benefits of mindfulness for equestrians can be found in the table below.

> *Being mindful is attending to the present moment with intention and acceptance.*

Rider in balance

> *Mindfulness for equestrians; the benefits of staying mindfully aware with your horse:*
>
> - *Better flow in the session*
> - *Noticing things you hadn't noticed before*
> - *Increased closeness and understanding of each other's cues*
> - *Skillful, refined, and flexible response to your horse's behaviours*
> - *Noticing your physical state and being able to stay physically balanced*
> - *Creating emotional balance for yourself*
> - *Being kinder to yourself and improving the quality of time with your horse*
> - *Enabling your horse to retain their innate emotional balance*
>
> *Together, these benefits generate improved communication and connection between you and your horse.*

Exercises and activities in this book

The exercises in the second half of this book are designed to flexibly meet your needs and should be suitable for all readers, with this caveat: *we assume that you are familiar with safe horse handling or are being supervised by an experienced mentor*. We also encourage you to actively take care of your horse and yourself when attempting any of the exercises. We talk further about this in Chapter 3, and we *strongly recommend* reviewing that content *before* attempting any of the exercises.

We have grouped the exercises into four main themes: sensory, equestrian activity-focused, cognitive/emotional, and relationship. As mentioned, we also provide you with the guided audio versions and videos of these exercises to offer full benefit. These are accessible at www.mindfulmarewellness.com.

You may find it helpful to practise the exercises in the sequence in which they are presented to progressively strengthen your mindfulness skills.

On the other hand, you may find that it suits your style or needs to select exercises from the areas that most interest you or because of your prior experience. We do recommend looking at the Foundation Exercise *prior* to trying other exercises in the book, since it provides a base from which to deepen your mindfulness practice. You can practise the same exercise on different occasions with the same or different horses. With each exercise, we suggest ways in which you can modify it over time—whether in a different equestrian context or in different life situations. This could be at work or at home, and with or without your horse.

As you become familiar with the material and practise it regularly, your mindful awareness will grow. We invite you to be with what *is* and not strive to get anywhere in this process, which can be different than our usual approach to life's demands.

In most of the exercises in this book, the practice will focus on one thing at a time. Although horses can notice many things at once, it will be easier for you to develop mindfulness skills if you start small, before expanding awareness to focus on several events occurring at once.

Although this may be a shift of routine for you and your horse, we encourage you to be open-minded and to remember that there are no limits to how much you can learn about yourself and your horse.

There are some guiding principles for the exercises in this book:

- The exercises and discussion in this book build on our belief that *horses are sentient beings*, with a unique consciousness and emotional awareness.

- We are dedicated to ensuring that *no harm* arises from these exercises. None of the exercises are meant to worsen quality of life for either you or your horse; rather, we hope that these exercises will help to *enhance* both well-being and the sense of connection between you, as dual sentient beings. We offer some tips how to respond to human or equine distress in descriptions of individual exercises.

- Remember that this book is not intended to replace counselling and/or psychotherapy.

> *We have a responsibility to take care of our horses no matter what we are doing with them.*

This book is intended as an invitation to try something different with your horse. It is an exploration of a different way of being in the presence of your horse, meeting them where they are, and tuning in to what they are trying to communicate to you. Through this process, we hope that you get to know yourself better, have more fun with your horse, and perceive other personal benefits such as improved attention and working memory.

This is not a training manual, a book from which to learn groundwork or "start" your horse. Other books exist for such purposes, and we encourage you to seek them out. This is a book to help you *BE* with your horse, which can be incredibly rewarding. While this is not a goal-directed journey, we hope that you find several surprises and learning opportunities along the way. It is our hope that the exercises in this book will be a first step in developing your own equine mindfulness connection. Enjoy!

The journey begins

Sharing the Present

Erich and Joe, Amanda Ubell Photography

References and resources

Sources cited

Gehrke, E. K. (2013). "The Horse-Human Heart Connection: Results of Studies using Heart Rate Variability." Accessed September 26, 2020: http://www.mindfulhorsemindfulleader.com/wp-content/uploads/2013/01/Research_The-Horse-Human-Heart-Connection-1.pdf

Low, Philip. (2012). "The Cambridge Declaration of Consciousness." Accessed September 26, 2020, from http://fcmconference.org/img/CambridgeDeclarationOnConsciousness.pdf

McFarland, C., Parelli, L., & Parelli, P. (2011). "When Emotions Affect Your Horse Relationship." Accessed September 26, 2020: http://www.midsouthhorsereview.com/news.php?id=4414

Shapiro, S. L., & Carlson, L. E. (2009). *The Art and Science of Mindfulness: Integrating Mindfulness into Psychology and the Helping Professions*. Washington, DC: American Psychological Association Press.

Smith, A. V., Proops, L., Grounds, K., Wathan, J., & McComb, K. (2016). "Functionally relevant responses to human facial expressions of emotion in the domestic horse (Equus caballus)." *Biology Letters*, 12(2), 1–4. https://royalsocietypublishing.org/doi/10.1098/rsbl.2015.0907

Additional references from this chapter

Rhonda Bignell. Owner and Riding Coach, Hawkstone Stables. Spruce Grove, AB.

Rick Warren. (2012). Day 19, "Cultivating Community." *The Purpose Driven Life: What on Earth am I Here For?* [10th anniversary edition]. Nashville, TN: HarperCollins Christian Publishing.

Equine training resources

Cummings, P. (2013). *Connected Riding: An Introduction.* Denver, CO: Outskirts Press, Inc.

Swift, S. (1985). *Centered Riding.* New York, NY: St. Martin's Press.

Tellington-Jones, L. (2006). *The Ultimate Horse Behavior and Training Book: Enlightened and Revolutionary Solutions for the 20th Century.* Pomfret, VT: Trafalgar Square Books.

Equine-facilitated wellness and animal sentience resources

de Waal, F. B. M. (2019). *Mama's Last Hug: Animal Emotions and What They Tell Us about Ourselves.* New York, NY: W. W. Norton & Company.

Dunning, A. (with Kohanov, L.). (2017). *The Horse Leads the Way: Honoring the True Role of the Horse in Equine Facilitated Practice.* Bishop's Castle, England: YouCaxton Publications.

Beholding Grace, SJ Originals Photography

CHAPTER 2
Understanding Mindfulness

"The sooner we let go of the idea that horses think like humans, the sooner we will start to make headway with our relationships with our horses."
~~ Cheryl Kimball

"It takes time, grace for self and others, and often many missteps along the way to learn and adopt a new way of being. If we allow them, horses can be wonderful teachers and role models in this."
~~ Sue McIntosh

Mindfulness is a term that describes a particular state of awareness, one in which you actively notice—with particular attitudes—things that are happening to you, around you, or within you. To say you are "being mindful" means that you are paying attention in a mindful way. When you consistently spend time practising this attentive awareness, you tune in more often to the present moment, rather than dwelling on the past or the future. This chapter offers theory on mindful awareness that will complement your personal learnings when experimenting with the exercises in Section 2.

Although mindfulness originated from certain spiritual practices, secular mindfulness ideas have now been incorporated into various psychotherapies to enhance the lives of those who are healthy and to assist those with chronic pain, anxiety, or depression. We describe secular mindfulness ideas in this book.

> *Have you had moments in life when you've been fully immersed in the present moment? Perhaps this experience sounds familiar. Everyone has this innate ability for mindfulness—a skill that is strengthened through regular practice.*

The mindfulness descriptions in this section are influenced by our personal experiences as well as the mindfulness literature by several writers and teachers:

- Dr. Jon Kabat-Zinn, who created Mindfulness-Based Stress Reduction (MBSR) therapy
- Dr. Marsha Linehan, who developed Dialectical Behavior Therapy (DBT)
- Thich Nhat Hanh, an internationally renowned mindfulness practitioner, teacher, and a Vietnamese Buddhist monk who has lived much of his life in Europe and the United States

For those readers who wish to learn more about these topics, please see the reference list at the end of this chapter.

Horses are mindful role models

As mentioned in the last chapter, horses are excellent role models for showing us how to live in the present. Observing how horses live their lives is one way to understand mindfulness. They don't think about yesterday's news, paying the bills, or getting the laundry done. They don't mull over that conversation they had with the new co-worker at the office or whether they will be able to get through Saturday's to-do list. They don't spend their days wondering when they'll get their next treat, when they will next sleep in the barn, or about the time earlier in the day when they were nipped by another horse in the field (contrary to appearances at times). Rather than getting caught up in past or future, they are wholly absorbed in *right now*. If you can access a similar state of mind, even for *some* of the time, you are moving in the direction of a calmer, more settled life.

In the next illustration, you see a horse and her human walking together thinking quite different thoughts. Even if your mind is full, like that of the person in the illustration, you can be as mindful as the horse is in the illustration. What do we mean by that? Does that mean we want you to empty your mind of thoughts? Not at all. Mindfulness is about noticing and accepting what is, without judgment. We are not suggesting that you must empty your mind of thoughts or that you must have a quiet mind to be mindful; in fact, in mindfulness meditation, you are invited to notice what is happening for you right now. If there are many thoughts or emotions in your present moment, then that is your experience right now. If your mind is full, you can still be mindfully present. There is no right or wrong way to experience the present moment. What we are suggesting is that, with regular practice, you can intentionally shift attention away from thoughts if that is not your desired focal point for attention. In other words, mindful practice allows for choice – where to place, maintain or shift attention over time.

> Remember, you can be mindful regardless of whether your mind is busy or quiet. The key is actively noticing your present moment experience so that you can choose where to place attention. When you are mind-full, however, you can get stuck in stuff such that you cannot choose where to place attention.

Mind Full vs. Mindful, posted with permission from Horse South Australia

What do I pay attention to?

To *be in the present moment*, try focusing on any of the following:

- The five senses—noticing sights, sounds, tastes, smells, and touch (i.e., anything you are in physical contact with) offers you a powerful way to stay anchored in the present. This helps you to maintain a link to your surrounding environment.

- Breath sensations in your body—noticing how the air moves in and out of your entire body or focusing on breathing sensations in certain areas, such as at the nostrils, back of the throat, the chest or abdomen

- Other bodily sensations—attending to either your whole body or specific parts of it

- Other events in your experience—paying attention to thoughts, emotions, or feelings

- More complex events—focusing on your communication and relationships with others, which becomes possible after further practice

This inventory of what to pay attention to when practising mindfulness skills is a good starting point. Often, you can start by simply attending to *one thing at a time*. However, another way to be mindful is paying attention to *several things at once*. When practising in this way, you intentionally notice whatever arises in the present moment, in one moment after the other, including environmental cues, bodily sensations, thoughts, emotions, or anything else. This multiple focus is often more challenging though, so starting with an individual focus can be helpful before attempting to expand your awareness to several things at once. Some people choose to practise focusing on only one thing at a time for their entire mindfulness journey and still find this beneficial.

Being able to stay mindful with a multiple focus is not the same as multitasking, which often occurs distractedly. Our exercises allow for a gradual strengthening of mindfulness skills so that you become progressively more capable of noticing a single (or various) event arising in the present moment. Although we have said that you aren't striving to get somewhere, remember that the more you practice the more your skills will develop. Even if you cannot be as skillful as your horse (who does this naturally), setting the intention to try this way of being in their presence is a beginning.

> *It's easy to feel pressured to multi-task in a distractible way, rather than focusing fully on just one thing in the present moment. Reflect on how your animals teach you about living in the present.*

Mindfulness and mindful attitudes

When we practise mindfulness, we pay attention in select ways to things as they happen. These approaches are called the "mindful attitudes." As we describe these attitudes below, we encourage you to think about how they apply to your time with your horse. You could also consider how such attitudes may be nurtured in everyday situations outside of the barn environment.

1. Non-judgment

The only real mistake is the one from which we learn nothing.
~~Henry Ford

When paying attention mindfully to the here and now, even if you don't like what you are noticing, you are staying aware in a non-judgmental way. Why does this matter? Because noticing things in this way makes it possible to see reality unfolding, right now, in a more accurate way.

Being non-judgmental goes hand in hand with being open and curious about everything arising in the present moment—just as it is. For example, if you decide to notice your bodily sensations in this way, then you notice both the relaxed *and* the tense feelings, along with any painful areas of your body. You notice all these things in *exactly the same way*—without judgment. You practise accepting what arises in each moment, rather than clinging to certain things or pushing others away. Equestrians can also apply this non-judgmental attitude when they are paying attention to their horses, whether they are grooming, practising a simple ridden movement or pattern, or working on a more complicated routine.

> *Remember that all these skills take practice.*

To help demonstrate the idea of being non-judgmental, we want to share a detailed account of working with our previous horse, Arya, who we adopted from a rescue foundation. Learning from and training horses is indeed a lifelong journey. Arya was about 14 years old at the time we knew her, and she had been left in a pasture with a fellow mare for a fair amount of time. This meant that she was relatively isolated from people when she was younger, and as a result, she displayed "herd-bound" behaviours. This is a term used to describe anxiety-driven, attachment-based behaviours that horses display when they feel threatened when they are away from their herd—in particular, when they are away from a specific buddy in the herd (Scholl, 2014). Owing to other early experiences, Arya also tended to resort to kicking when she felt scared in a new situation.

When she first arrived, Arya was quarantined in her own paddock. We knew we had to work on creating a relationship of trust with her from scratch. We spent time grooming and talking to her. We practised basic groundwork manners and exercises. Over multiple sessions, we noticed that she became more trusting of us, more responsive to our cues, and she quickly relaxed and was attentive during the sessions. As with any experience involving horses, there were good days and bad days. Overall, things were progressing.

> *Herd-bound behaviour*
>
> These are anxiety-driven behaviours that a horse displays if they feel threatened when they are away from their herd—in particular, when they are away from a specific buddy in the herd.

Arya with Rhonda, Next to Wild Photography

Arya with Rhonda (2), Next to Wild Photography

Shreyasi and Arya coached by Rhonda, Next to Wild Photography

Shreyasi and Arya coached by Rhonda (2), Next to Wild Photography

When her quarantine was complete, she was turned out with other horses. When we brought her in for her next session, she began to demonstrate her herd-bound tendencies. She was distracted and whinnying, and her eyes constantly sought out her herd buddies. We experienced disconnected moments unlike what was experienced previously. We had to frequently remind Arya to pay attention and follow our cues. Further, we had to assert ourselves when she tried to run through us to get to her buddies. We had to be swift enough to get out of the way of potential kicks or other stress-driven behaviours, while asserting our presence at other times as leader. The session did not flow as well as we'd expected given the previous successful sessions.

So, how can mindfulness help us in such situations? If we apply mindfulness to the example of working with Arya, we commit to being completely tuned in to each moment, *even if we don't like it.*

Overwhelming emotions can arise in sessions like this one. You might start thinking of past sessions that have been successful and how different this session is. Fear might become your focus through the session, as you notice the potentially dangerous behaviours in your horse. You might worry about the future, think poorly of your skills or the horse's abilities, and so on. It would be easy to label your horse (or yourself) in a negative way during a session like this, and it is worth noting that labels originating from a place of judgment are usually inaccurate. For example, labelling Arya as "difficult," or getting harsh with ourselves could have led to feeling shut down, insecure, and unable to notice what else was happening in the session. An alternative approach is to notice what arises, be kind with yourself, and explore the situation with curiosity.

In this example, staying non-judgmental helped us to identify that one possible explanation for Arya's changed behaviour was anxiety due to being away from the herd and not feeling safe in our presence. When we aren't taking things personally, we can reflect on the various possibilities in a situation.

Arya's behaviours could, alternatively, have been related to testing boundaries, and this may have accounted for her behaviour in this session. Again, if we get stuck in judging ourselves for viewing her in this way, we may avoid exploring this possible explanation for her behaviour. Readers with horse experience may consider still other reasons for her behaviour in this session.

There are many reasons for a horse to behave in a particular way at a specific time and within a certain environment. Mindful awareness skills can help you to step away from being overwhelmed by your horse's behaviours. Instead, you can notice your emotions and what they indicate about the situation you are in, let go of judgments about these feelings or yourself, and tune in accurately to events arising in the present. Staying connected to present moment happenings in this way better facilitates problem-solving and may even change the situation for the better. If you notice you are judging something, stay patient with yourself and return your focus to what can be done differently *right now*. This allows both you and your horse to make a shift to more "successful" behaviours. Although we are breaking down the steps here for you, they will happen quickly in real-life situations as you continue to practise.

From a safety perspective, becoming aware of what is happening in the present moment allows you to detect the swish of a tail, the ears pinned back, or the horse's bodily tension, and to respond in a timely manner. This helps you to stay safe if things escalate. Staying fully aware of events unfolding in each moment makes all the difference in potentially unsafe situations.

> *Overthinking or judging yourself and your horse can take you away from the present moment, which is the only moment in which positive change can occur.*

Opportunities emerge so that we may learn and grow from both the "good" and the "bad" times. The challenge is to be open and embrace the full range of experiences presented to you; we know this is not always easy. If you notice you are judging what you are observing or feeling, you can deliberately focus on other aspects of the present and move them to the foreground of awareness:

- Notice your horse's body language
- Keep track of what you are asking your horse to do
- Monitor how you reinforce horse behaviours through your actions and words
- Pay attention to other things you notice in the session

This process of noticing where your mind is and intentionally bringing your attention back to focus on the task at hand is what mindfulness is all about. People often think that to be mindful they should *always* be focused on one thing, but this isn't how the human brain works. Rather, the very act of noticing when the mind is distracted and then refocusing attention is part of being mindfully tuned in to the present moment.

> *A mindful process: Notice → Accept where your mind is → Refocus*

It is often hard *not* to judge yourself for judging! This is so common because everyone wants to do the best they can for their horse. The maxim here is: *No one* is perfect. We are *all* learning. Most people will fall into judging themselves at some point or another, but it is helpful to remember that, in the end, this doesn't help.

Sharing the Present

Violet and Lucky, Prairie Darkroom Photography

2. Beginner's mind

Treating each session as a fresh start and remembering that no session is completely the same as the one before exemplifies this second mindful attitude. The "beginner's mind" perspective makes it simpler for you to remain focused on the present experience every time you are with your horse. Without a doubt, this is easier said than done—to imagine and act as if each time you see your horse, it is the first time. Everyone naturally forms expectations, over time, about familiar situations. We encourage you to remember that your *expectations* and *memories* are not as accurate as the facts unfolding before you in the present moment. Unfortunately, if you become too stuck on what you expect, you miss out on the crucial information available in the moment.

> *One way to understand "beginner's mind" is this quote by Allison Trimble: "Treat each new day like a freshly worked arena: free of the footprints from yesterday's ride."*

Thus, beginner's mind makes it possible to:

1. Notice quickly what a session with your horse is turning into, then responding actively to deal with the facts of the current moment.

2. Notice when your horse is exhibiting desired behaviours.

3. Reward the horse's efforts as often as possible (also called "rewarding the try").

4. Decide whether to continue practising the desired behaviour.

5. Decide to try something else with your horse in the session.

When you take a mindful approach to the time that you spend with your horse, you spend less time in your head—thinking, planning, assessing, remembering, and so on—and more time sensing and responding to what is happening in front of you. This helps you to stay observant and connected to your horse. Instead of "holding on" to your past knowledge of a particular horse, we ask you to stay curious about how your horse is in the present moment and to be open to possibilities. The goal is to help you see your horse exactly as they are and to avoid getting stuck in preconceived notions or assumptions. This is paying attention with a *beginner's mind*.

If this is difficult to understand, remember that horses naturally show us examples of a beginner's mind every day. When you spend time around horses, you may notice that they treat each day as a fresh start. This does not imply that horses cannot be shaped by past experiences or remember prior learning, but rather that they can enter a situation while being fully aware that this immediate moment is a new experience. They are great role models of all these mindful attitudes.

3. Acceptance and compassion

Being accepting and compassionate during mindfulness practice means that you aren't fighting with the way things truly are. When you are accepting and compassionate of yourself, you can note whatever is happening and consciously decide to work with it just the way it is. Being attentive to things in a compassionate way can be hard to understand. You may have noticed that we describe paying attention with kindness or staying gentle with yourself when you notice judgments—this is a way of expressing self-compassion during mindful awareness.

Another way of saying this is to give yourself a break when you feel critical of yourself or your horse. We are often more supportive of others than ourselves. You can model self-compassion during any of the exercises in this book or at any time you are with your horse. Mistakes can happen, things can be misunderstood, and this is all part of the lifelong learning that every horse owner experiences.

> *There is real strength in being compassionate. It takes courage to forgive yourself and your horse and to stay kind even during times of disappointment.*

When you notice that you are being critical of yourself or of your horse, it is a cue to switch to a gentler approach towards both of you. This is one way of expressing *grace*. Staying critical and harsh isn't helpful, and these intense emotions fill up your awareness, making it hard to focus on anything else that is happening in the moment. Everyone goes through challenges and struggles, and the key is to work through these situations without judging. We believe that you can be compassionate to yourself and your horse while at the same time adopting the role of a fair and calm leader.

The idea of self-compassion has been researched by Dr. Kristin Neff, who identified three core elements that contribute to this phenomenon. The summary below comes from Dr. Brené Brown's book, *The Gifts of Imperfection* (2010):

> Self-kindness: Being warm and understanding towards ourselves when we suffer, fail, or feel inadequate, rather than ignoring our pain or flagellating ourselves with self-criticism.
>
> Common humanity: Common humanity recognizes that suffering and feelings of personal inadequacy are part of the shared human experience—something we all go through, rather than something that happens to "me" alone.
>
> Mindfulness: Taking a balanced approach to negative emotions so that feelings are neither suppressed nor exaggerated. We cannot ignore our pain and feel compassion for it at the same time. Mindfulness requires that we not "over-identify" with thoughts and feelings, so that we are caught up and swept away by negativity. (pp. 59-60)

Noticing what arises in the moment is the first step to staying compassionate of our experiences. There are always opportunities to remember you are not alone during challenging times. This is a large part of why we seek out other like-minded individuals to generate a supportive and nurturing horse community around us. Given what is already known about people's emotional impact on horses, being kind to yourself in the presence of these empathic beings likely helps them to partner with us during tough moments.

Sharing the Present

Compassion

4. Letting go

"Letting go" has several meanings, but for the purpose of mindfulness practice, it refers to the general approach of noticing things, holding them for a while in your present attention, and then releasing them to focus on something else happening in the present moment.

When you practise this attitude, you experience the present moment as if you are an observer. You can watch events (like physical sensations, thoughts, and feelings) arise and pass in each moment without getting caught up or letting them wholly occupy your attention. With regular practice, you can flexibly shift attention to any event in the present moment while letting other parts of the present-moment experience, such as thoughts or feelings, remain in the background. The thoughts or feelings do not have to be the primary focus, unless you choose them to be so (we practise noticing thoughts and emotions in a later exercise in the book).

The imaginary container, as mentioned in Chapter 1, is a useful way to envision this. Imagine placing your thoughts or emotions into a container and then setting the container aside for a moment, knowing that you can open and explore the contents later. The goal is to develop your capacity to choose *when* to attend to your thoughts and emotions, rather than your thoughts and emotions taking over. We talk about this more in Chapter 3, to cope with overwhelming thoughts and feelings. You can also try the two metaphor exercises described in the box below.

> *These visual metaphors help you to understand the process of letting go.*
>
> ### Riverbank Metaphor
>
> Imagine that you are standing on the edge of a river and watching the water flow by. As you stand on the riverbank, observing the water, imagine that the river contains thoughts and emotions arising in the moment. Standing there, you can observe the thoughts and emotions, as they flow along the water.
>
> An alternative but related image is to visualize your thoughts and emotions as clouds in the sky. You can watch them pass, just as you might watch the clouds float by.

Sharing the Present

Conveyor Belt Metaphor

In this scenario, imagine your thoughts and emotions being inside boxes or crates that pass you on a conveyor belt—without taking them off the belt. This is akin to mindfully observing your thoughts and emotions without getting caught up in them. You can label the boxes or thoughts as "a worry thought," "a thought about the past," "a question," and so forth. You might explore the thoughts by taking certain boxes off the conveyor belt and opening them to see what's inside. Just remember to put them back on the belt when you're done.

Riverbank

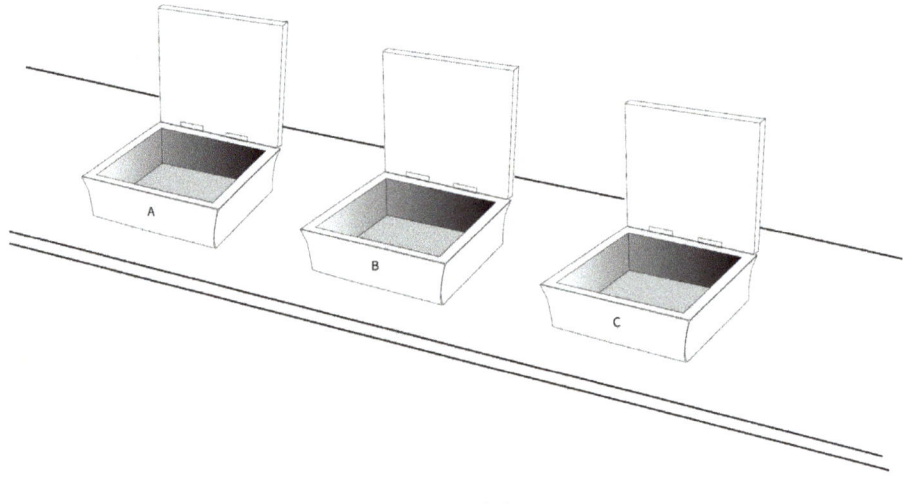

Conveyor belt

The attitude of letting go can apply to working with horses in many ways. One way is to let go of thoughts and emotions from earlier in the day, if possible, before seeing your horse. This is something that Frank likes to call "cleansing." Another way is letting go of the events of a previous session, so it frees you up to have a fresh start and open mind ("beginner's mind") for the next time you are with your horse. The art of letting go can also determine when to end a training session with your horse. For example, there are times when you should continue your session to allow your horse to learn a new behaviour, and there are other times that your horse may be struggling with a concept. It may be better, in this instance, to end the session on a positive note by returning to something that they are comfortable doing and have had previous success with. The flexibility that comes with letting go helps you to make these choices during everyday interactions with your horse. These decisions may initially require some support from your trainer or coach until you are more comfortable on your own.

> *Letting go does not mean that you forget things that you've learned before. Rather, you are making space for new learning to occur.*

Another way to practise letting go is during those times when you have self-doubts while you are with your horse. When you're in a tough spot, emotionally or otherwise, being able to let go helps you respond more effectively. For instance, if you doubt yourself or think that you will never connect with your horse in the way that you want to, you can tell yourself something like this:

I am noticing thoughts and/or feelings of doubt right now. What do I want to do with this information? Shall I keep analyzing this, focus on something else, or problem-solve in some way? Is there something I must learn to accept in this case? Shall I ask someone else for help?

Letting go can also be about saying goodbye, which is a hard and unavoidable part of any horse-human relationship. There is an exercise later in this book which is intended to help you face the emotions of letting go in this way and to cope with the feelings of saying goodbye.

Letting go

> 🐎 *Develop mindfulness with practice through these four mindful attitudes:*
>
> - *Being non-judgmental*
> - *Having a beginner's mind*
> - *Developing acceptance and practising compassion (to events and to oneself)*
> - *Letting go*

Building your mindfulness capacity

Being mindful with the horses, photograph by Jennifer Maciej

Sensing, not thinking

As you practise the mindfulness exercises in the second half of this book, the distinction between sensing and thinking will become clear. First-hand experience is often the best way to get inside this abstract concept. You can't simply think about your breath, or your body, or your horse. Instead, you have to *feel* all these things. Mindfulness steps around thinking or over-thinking and, instead, elevates sensing and feeling as the means to navigate your way through experiences.

Getting distracted

As you work through the exercises, remember that *it is completely normal not to focus on the present all the time.* Your mind will sometimes wander into events of the past or future, and it may be difficult to focus on some aspect of the present due to the everyday distractions of the environment around you. Thoughts of the past or future are typically considered distractions in mindfulness practice since we are paying primary attention to aspects of the present moment besides thoughts, such as breathing or our senses. However, if you are intentionally paying attention to thoughts or emotions in this moment (as we do later in this book), then noticing that the mind veers into the past or the future may be exactly what you are choosing to notice right now. It really depends on what your chosen focus of attention is in this moment.

One way to pull your focus into the present moment (regardless of your chosen focus of attention) is by picking *one specific thing* in the present and noting how that *one thing* changes from one moment to the next. This could be the sensation of your breathing; a physical sensation in a certain part of your body, such as your feet on the ground or your back against a chair; or what you are sensing with any one of your five senses. For example, you could ask yourself these questions to centre your focus:

- What am I seeing right now?
- What am I hearing right now?
- What am I feeling through touch right now?

It's also common to be distracted from your chosen focus of attention in the present moment if there are certain judgments, uncomfortable physical sensations, or emotions that occupy your attention. In such situations, notice where your attention is placed and then return your focus to whatever you are trying to pay attention to *right now*. This process of noticing distractions and returning your attention back to the task at hand *builds your mindfulness skills*. The thoughts and feelings might still be there in the background while we attend to something else. We offer suggestions on shifting attention away from intense thoughts and emotions in Chapter 3. (Remember that the only time we do not shift attention away from thoughts and emotions is when we are practising to intentionally notice them, as we do later in this book.)

Autopilot

Being attentive to what happens, as it is happening, is the opposite of what is sometimes called "autopilot." Autopilot is when people go through the motions of a task without paying full attention. Most people spend significant periods of the day in this state. For example, you might drive to work or to a friend's house and have little or no recollection of the drive, an insight that may dawn on you only after you arrive. This is usually because you weren't fully attentive to driving and your mind was occupied, instead, with other thoughts or reflections. In the "autopilot" frame of mind, you miss out on things that you might want to pay attention to in the moment.

We have already talked about how, with Arya and our other horses, if we are distracted and not truly in the present—if we are in autopilot mode—we miss out on important messages in our horses' body language. This has potentially dangerous consequences, since by missing key physical cues, such as distress or irritation from our horse (tail swishing, ears pinned back, tension in the jaw, and so on), we could get pushed, kicked, or otherwise harmed.

Informal mindfulness

This book focuses on helping to build everyday mindfulness, also called *informal mindfulness*, through exercises related to your relationship and interaction with horses. The informal mindfulness exercises in this book will help you to build your mindfulness skills when practised regularly. They can also improve the relationship between you and your horse—as we have found from our own experience. Some readers may have heard that mindfulness is another word to describe meditation. While various mindfulness-based therapies do use some meditation practices, you don't have to meditate to be mindful. You can be mindful in any moment. It is noteworthy that many in the mindfulness field promote the benefits of *informal mindfulness*.

Less than perfect is okay

There are no goals or grades that you need to achieve with mindful awareness exercises, and there is no perfect way to be mindful. Yes, paying attention mindfully is a skill you can strengthen with practice. But you won't ever be 100% mindful all the time. It is physiologically impossible.

Some days, being focused on the present may feel easy and natural, while on other days, it may feel incredibly challenging. As much as possible, practise these exercises with your horse while keeping an open mind rather than expecting them to go a certain way.

> *Although mindfulness can help you feel more alive, it is not something you can do 100% of the time, no matter how much you practise. And that is okay.*

Research on mindfulness

Mindfulness has been researched extensively over the past decades. The details of these studies are outside the scope of this book; however, we include a summary of some key findings in this section to illustrate that being mindful has evidence-based personal benefits.

Mindfulness meditation and mindfulness-based psychotherapies have been tested in various age groups, in both healthy individuals and in those suffering from chronic mental health and physical conditions. In the last 10 to 15 years, these studies have been numerous and wide-ranging in their focus, including several mindfulness treatments, such as those mentioned in Chapter 1. Dialectical Behavior Therapy, or DBT, is a *mindfulness-related therapy*, while Mindfulness-Based Stress Reduction (MBSR) and Mindfulness-Based Cognitive Therapy (MBCT) are both considered to be *mindfulness-based therapies*.

Several studies have explored the effects of mindfulness meditation on thinking or functioning in people without mental health diagnoses, such as the following:

- *Brain structure:* Mindfulness may alter regions of the brain to improve brain function and reduce stress.

- *Various tasks related to processes of attention, working memory, or decision-making (known as "executive functioning"):* Mindfulness can enhance one's attention span and working memory.

- *Ratings of positive or negative emotional states (also known as positive and negative "affect"):* Mindfulness may help to regulate emotions or recover from negative emotions in healthy individuals.

- *Ratings of self-reported stress, and burnout:* Mindfulness decreases stress and alleviates burnout in healthy individuals.

- *Clinical rating scores on scales of depression and anxiety:* For those who are clinically depressed or anxious, as measured on clinical rating scales, scores improved immediately after completing a mindfulness meditation intervention, compared to those on a waitlist or in a control group.

Often, to determine the impact of mindfulness, researchers compare the ratings of participants (for example, pertaining to mood, working memory, and so forth) before and after they complete a mindfulness-based program. Alternatively, they may compare the results of those who completed the mindfulness program with those who are on a waitlist or enrolled in another type of therapy program. Findings show that in the absence of other major mental health concerns, even brief mindfulness meditation practice—such as fifteen minutes a day for at least eight weeks—can have a beneficial impact.

In broad terms, researchers have found evidence that mindfulness-based interventions offer benefits to people experiencing a range of conditions, such as:

- Attention Deficit Hyperactivity Disorder (ADHD)
- Chronic depression
- Generalized anxiety
- Sleep disturbance
- Chronic pain
- Fibromyalgia
- Breast cancer
- Multiple sclerosis

Specific mindfulness therapies, such as MBSR and MBCT, have been associated with participants reporting fewer events of chronic pain, anxiety, and depression, as measured on clinical rating scales. MBCT stands out as being a useful treatment for people who've had several episodes of depression in the past, by reducing the risk for further episodes and preventing relapse. Mindfulness as part of DBT can reduce self-harm behaviours in individuals with borderline personality disorder (although there are several additional components to this treatment, of course). We list the pertinent studies in the reference list at the end of this chapter, and you can review the details and results of these studies, if you choose. See especially Shapiro and Carlson (2009) for a synopsis.

Summary

We hope this chapter has provided you with a summary of what it means to be mindful and to practise this type of awareness regularly. It is extremely hard to describe mindfulness in words. The only way to understand what we mean in this chapter is by trying the exercises to see what happens for you. Like any new skill being learned, it may seem hard at first. The more you practise, the easier it is to be mindful.

The paradox is that mindfulness practice can strengthen your skills in mindfulness, even though it is a process without any specific goals. Many parallels to this concept exist in nature, ranging from the bud that blossoms into a flower to the egg hatching into a fledgling, or to the butterfly that unfurls its wings after a process of metamorphosis from a chrysalis. In all these instances, growth happens when things are left to be as they are and to evolve at their natural pace. So it is with mindfulness practice and the growing capacity to be aware of present events while they are happening.

You may have questions based on the content in this chapter, and we encourage you to revisit them after trying the exercises. Your questions may be answered through your actual experiences, and if not, you are welcome to contact us or access other mindfulness-based resources for guidance. As we are not there, in person, to facilitate you through these exercises, we have made every effort to make them accessible and "practise friendly." We encourage you to contact us if you have questions or comments on how you or your horse respond to the exercises. We have placed videos and guided audio exercises on our website, www.mindfulmarewellness.com, to show you another view of these exercises. We also include a list of mindfulness-based resources below.

References and resources

Herd-bound behaviours

Scholl, K. (2014). "*Herd Bound Behavior – Part 1.*" Retrieved from https://equinewellnessmagazine.com/herd-bound-behaviour-part-1/

Self-Compassion reference

Brown, B. (2010). *The Gifts of Imperfection: Let Go of Who You Think You're Supposed to Be and Embrace Who You Are.* Center City, MN: Hazelden Publishing.

Mindfulness resources

Books

Hanh, T. N. (1991). *Peace Is Every Step: The Path of Mindfulness in Everyday Life.* New York, NY: Bantam Books.

Hanh, T. N. (1999). *The Miracle of Mindfulness: An Introduction to the Practice of Meditation.* Boston, MA: Beacon Press.

Kabat-Zinn, J. (2004). *Wherever You Go, There You Are: Mindfulness Meditation in Everyday Life.* London, England: Piatkus.

Kabat-Zinn, J. (2018). *Falling Awake: How to Practice Mindfulness in Everyday Life.* New York, NY: Hachette Books.

Salzberg, S. (2002). *Loving-kindness: The Revolutionary Art of Happiness* (revised ed.). Boulder, CO: Shambhala.

Exercises and other suggestions for practice

Kaiser Greenland, S., & Harris, A. (2017). *Mindful Games Activity Cards: 55 Fun Ways to Share Mindfulness with Kids and Teens.* Boulder, CO: Shambhala.

Snel, E. (2013). *Sitting Still Like a Frog: Mindfulness Exercises for Kids (and Their Parents)*. Boulder, CO: Shambhala.

Stewart, W., & Braun, M. (2017). *Mindful Kids: 50 Mindfulness Activities for Kindness, Focus and Calm*. Cambridge, MA: Barefoot Books.

Willard, C., & Abblett, M. (2016). *Mindfulness Reminders Card Deck: 52 Powerful Practices for Adults*. Eau Claire, WI: Pesi Publishing & Media.

Willey, K. (2017). *Breathe Like a Bear: 30 Mindful Moments for Kids to Feel Calm and Focused Anytime, Anywhere*. New York, NY: Rodale Kids.

Therapies

Kabat-Zinn, J. (1990). *Full Catastrophe Living: Using the Wisdom of Your Body and Mind to Face Stress, Pain, and Illness*. New York, NY: Delacourt.

Linehan, M. M. (2015a). *DBT Skills Training Manual* (2nd ed.). New York, NY: Guilford Press.

Linehan, M. M. (2015b). *DBT Skills Training Handouts and Worksheets* (2nd ed.). New York, NY: Guilford Press.

Shapiro, S. L., & Carlson, L. E. (2009). *The Art and Science of Mindfulness: Integrating Mindfulness into Psychology and the Helping Professions*. Washington, DC: American Psychological Association Press. [Chapters 5 and 6 are especially helpful].

Audio resources

Meditation downloads, including a lovingkindness meditation

http://self-compassion.org

http://www.mindfulselfcompassion.org

Meditation CDs

Kabat-Zinn, J. (2005). *Guided Mindfulness Meditation* [CD]. Louisville, CO: Sounds True Inc.

Kornfield, J. (2010). *Guided Meditations for Difficult Times: A Lamp in the Darkness* [CD]. Louisville, CO: Sounds True Inc.

Research on mindfulness and mindfulness-based therapies

Basso, J. C., McHale, A., Ende, V., Oberlin, D. J., & Suzuki, W. A. (2019). "Brief, daily meditation enhances attention, memory, mood, and emotional regulation in non-experienced meditators." *Behavioural Brain Research, 356,* 208–220.

Fountain-Zaragoza, S., & Prakash, R. S. (2017). "Mindfulness training for healthy aging: Impact on attention, well-being, and inflammation." *Frontiers in Aging Neuroscience*, 9(11), 1–15.

Gallant, S. N. (2016). "Mindfulness meditation practice and executive functioning: Breaking down the benefit." *Consciousness and Cognition, 40,* 116–130.

Goyal, M., Singh, S., Sibinga, E. M. S., Gould, N. F., Rowland-Seymour, A., Sharma, R., Berger, Z., … Haythornwaite, J. A. (2014). "Meditation programs for psychological stress and well-being: A systematic review and meta-analysis." *Journal of the American Medical Association, Internal Medicine,* 174(3), 57–368.

Hofmann, S. G., Grossman P., & Hinton, D. E. (2011). "Loving-kindness and compassion meditation: Potential for psychological interventions." *Clinical Psychology Review,* 31(7), 1126–32.

Khoo E. L., Small, R., Cheng, W., Hatchard, T., Glynn, B., Rice, D. B., … Poulin, P. A. (2019). "Comparative evaluation of group-based mindfulness-based stress reduction and cognitive behavioural therapy for the treatment and management of chronic pain: A systematic review and network meta-analysis." *Evidence-Based Mental Health*, 22(1), 26–35.

Khoury, B., Sharma, M., Rush, S. E., & Fournier, C. (2015). "Mindfulness-based stress reduction for healthy individuals: A meta-analysis." *Journal of Psychosomatic Research,* 78(6), 519–528.

Pascoe, M. C., Thompson, D. R., Jenkins, Z. M., & Ski C. F. (2017). "Mindfulness mediates the physiological markers of stress: Systematic review and meta-analysis." *Journal of Psychiatric Research, 95,* 156–178.

Shapiro, S. L., & Carlson, L. E. (2009). "Mindfulness-based interventions for mental health," in *The art and science of mindfulness: Integrating mindfulness into psychology and the helping professions.* [Chapters 5 and 6]. Washington, DC: American Psychological Association Press.

Tang, Y. Y., Holzel, B. K., & Posner M. I. (2015). "The neuroscience of mindfulness meditation." *Nature Reviews in Neuroscience, 16*(4), 13–225.

Braxton connecting with Rhianna, SJ Originals Photography

CHAPTER 3

Preparing for the Mindfulness Exercises with your Horse

Self-compassion is simply giving the same kindness to ourselves that we would give to others.

~~ Christopher Germer

There are two emotions that belong in the saddle; one is a sense of humour and the other is patience.

~~ John Lyons

Before you start the exercises in Section 2, we discuss how to take care of yourself and your horse during the process. When you first pay attention to present moment happenings, painful or overwhelming thoughts may arise. You may experience physical discomfort on occasion or notice signs of stress in your horse. In this chapter we offer strategies to respond to all these scenarios.

These exercises are not intended to harm you or your horse in any way. Please read this section before attempting the exercises, regardless of your level of experience with horses.

> *Mindful awareness exercises have both benefits and potential risks. One risk is unbearable emotional or physical distress during the process of noticing things exactly as they are in the present moment.*

Taking care of yourself by exploring your Window of Tolerance

When noticing what you feel *inside you*, in the present moment, you are noticing thoughts, emotions, bodily sensations, or a combination of these. If discomfort occurs, understanding your tolerance level helps you to respond. This is about knowing your Window of Tolerance.

The Window of Tolerance model was developed by Dr. Dan Siegel (1999). It is helpful to think of this window when you practise mindfulness exercises. Whenever you are in a new situation, your experience is either within your tolerance (where you learn and grow without being overwhelmed) or outside your tolerance (where you feel overwhelmed). Growth cannot happen in high stress states, rather it happens near the boundaries of our tolerance zone, where we challenge ourselves just a little without falling overboard into being overwhelmed.

We encourage you to remain within your window, rather than being overwhelmed, when you try these exercises. Whenever you are overwhelmed, select a strategy to return to feeling emotionally safe (we discuss these later in this chapter). Over time, your window of tolerance can expand with regular mindfulness practice. This allows you to attend to uncomfortable feelings, thoughts, or body sensations. But it is completely fine if that never happens.

> *You do not have to stay focused on painful thoughts and emotions to be mindful. You can be mindful even if you intentionally step away from them.*

After an exercise in which you felt overwhelmed, you can journal about what happened and/or share the experience with someone you trust. If you think your feelings or concerns are more serious, consider getting professional help to deal with them. This might include seeing a certified counsellor, social worker, psychologist, family physician, psychiatrist, or equine-facilitated wellness (EFW) professional.

Sharing the Present

Mindfully noticing uncomfortable thoughts and emotions

Uncomfortable thoughts can turn up during the mindfulness exercises and are hard to distract yourself from. They tend to "stick" and are typically associated with distressing emotions. Without you realizing it, these thoughts can affect your mood and influence your horse. So, it is helpful to attend to your thoughts with clarity.

"Sticky" thoughts can include:

- Regrets about the past
- Self-doubt
- Judgments of others
- Judgments of yourself
- Judgments of your horse
- Worries about the future

Sticky thoughts

> 🐎 *Thoughts and feelings are useful information to help you understand what's going on. You can't control when they turn up or leave, but you can control how you respond to them. This sets you free from their control.*

Uncomfortable emotions might be feelings of sadness, shame, frustration, disappointment, anxiety, or anything that makes you feel "stressed," "upset," or "depressed." When you start to use labels such as "stressed" or "upset," this usually means that you are feeling something intense, painful, or uncomfortable. You are amidst a strong emotion or mix of emotions.

Here are a few things to remember about thoughts and feelings/emotions:

- *Emotions are clues to understanding what is happening for you in a situation.* For example, you feel sad when you perceive a loss or experience an actual loss, you feel angry when you perceive that something unfair has happened to you or others, you feel scared when you perceive danger, or happy when you enjoy the moment. The meanings behind specific emotions, as described by Dr. Marsha Linehan, are found in her "Emotion Regulation Skills" module (see reference list in Chapter 2).

- *Bodily sensations can help you name or identify your emotions.* When you are feeling scared, you may notice sweaty palms, palpitations, or a queasy feeling in your stomach. When you feel sad, you may feel heaviness or aching in your chest. When you are happy, you may notice "lightness" and warm tingling. If you cannot tell what the emotions are by reading your body, it is useful to take a moment and reflect on the situation triggering the feelings. *What is happening? How are you interpreting this? What emotions might you feel in that case?* In this way, you use clues other than your bodily sensations to identify your emotions in a situation.

- *People sometimes get confused between their thoughts and emotions.* When you say, "I feel," this often means an emotion is coming up. For example, you might say, "I feel that this is not a good day," but this statement is really a *thought*. Your *feeling* might be frustration, disappointment, or something else, while your *thought* is: "This is not a good day for me."

> *When you mindfully notice your thoughts and emotions:*
>
> - You are less likely to feel overwhelmed, and you choose how to respond. Responding is different from reacting. When you respond, you are *aware* of what is happening and how you will act. This is different from reacting (that is, acting without awareness).
>
> - You can make changes to the situation, when possible, or learn to accept the way things are.
>
> - Once you have practised this with your horse, you can start applying it to other situations in your life, if you wish.

How can I deal with overwhelming thoughts or emotions during exercises?

If there are overwhelming thoughts or emotions, try one of these strategies to return to your healthy tolerance zone—that is, to your window of tolerance:

- *Breathe through the thought or emotion.* While breathing, tell yourself, "This is just a thought [or a feeling]. It will pass. I can handle this." Shift your attention to whatever you were paying attention to just before this came up.

- *Be your own cheerleader.* Give yourself positive encouragement through the tough moment.

- *Visualize the container* where you can temporarily store your feelings and deal with them later. Imagine the size, colour, texture, and appearance of the container; imagine placing the thoughts or emotions inside, sealing the container, and putting it away, for now. Remember that using the container is like using a pause button, not a delete, for these thoughts and emotions. You can open the container at another time.

- *Ground yourself back in your body* and out of your head. Grounding is connecting with your surroundings and your body to feel less overwhelmed. Try to:

- *Focus on your breathing.* Make yourself take deep breaths in and out.

- *Pay attention to one of your senses.* Notice what you are hearing, smelling, tasting, seeing, or touching, *right now*—either near your horse, or elsewhere. If there is nothing noticeable for a particular sense, then observe this and move on to the next sense. Or notice how it feels to have your feet touching the ground and the physical feeling of standing or sitting where you are.

- *Focus on listening to yourself counting out loud to 10.*

Grounding

- *Engage in movement.* Try walking, using alternating small or large steps, or tap your fingers in a rhythm as you focus on something other than the thought or emotion.

Sharing the Present

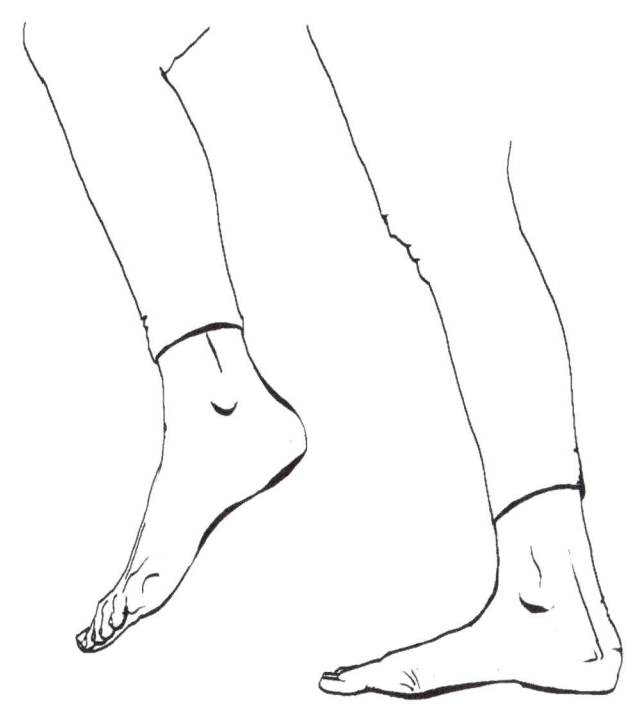

Soles of the feet

- *Take a short break if you start to feel scared.* You can take a break after ensuring that your horse is in a safe, enclosed area. Then return to what you were doing with your horse or share another activity with them. Returning to the barn is important to continue feeling safe there in future.

- *Practice self-soothing during or after the exercise.* Soothe your senses by giving yourself a hug or placing your hand gently over your heart. Or you could have a glass of water or pet the barn cat or dog before returning to your horse. Later in the day, you might smell a favourite essential oil, listen to soothing music, wrap yourself in a soft item of clothing, tell yourself things you might say to a close friend to comfort them in a similar situation, access spiritual practices important to you, or visualize being in a safe comforting place.

Have you tried any of these strategies before? What works for you when you are emotionally distressed? Perhaps you have tried other approaches to handle emotional stress that might be useful when you practise the exercises.

Shreyasi and Frank Brodhecker

Fiona in her field, Amanda Ubell Photography

Dealing with uncomfortable bodily sensations

You may find yourself dealing with uncomfortable physical sensations when you pay attention in the present moment. This may be in the form of cramps, aches, itchiness, or other uncomfortable bodily sensations. Here are some ideas for dealing with them:

- *Continue what you are doing.* Sometimes you can just notice the uncomfortable bodily sensation, let it be, and keep doing what you are doing.

- *Adjust your posture, stretch, or massage the sore area.* Sometimes this is all that is needed to relieve the sensation.

- *Take a break or go for a walk.* Getting away from the moment can change how you feel.

- *Focus on other physical sensations in the body.*

Only you can decide what's best for your body in this moment. See whether these or other things you try work for you.

A conscious shift in routine for you and your horse

When trying these exercises, it may seem confusing for you or your horse at first. This is a change from your usual routines together. Rather than getting something done, you are focusing on being with your horse. After you've tried these exercises a few times, you may notice less confusion. You might even start paying attention like this at other times that you spend with your horse. Being flexible will help you to feel more connected to your horse over time.

> *Can you be mindful even in brief moments of completing a task?*

Shreyasi and Frank Brodhecker

Connection, Next to Wild Photography

Taking care of your horse during the exercises

Just as we encourage taking care of yourself, we encourage taking care of your horse's physical and emotional safety. Remember that these exercises are intended to *strengthen* the connection between you and your horse and are entirely optional for you both.

Although you are *not* fully responsible for how your horse reacts in various situations, we *do* encourage you to pay close attention to the horse's physical and emotional states throughout. If you notice unease, you can show your horse calming signals (described later in this chapter), take a short break, and then try again, or just end the exercise. You can also practise some of the exercises on your own or try them again with the same horse or a different horse in future.

Being safe with your horse

If you are new to horses, please have an experienced person with you. Even if these exercises seem straightforward, we encourage you to practise them with support. This allows you and your horse to feel safe when trying something new.

We have included some common safety rules, created from our own experiences, and loosely based on Equestrian Canada Western and English Rider Levels (2017). It is a good idea to know how to safely turn your horse from side to side, stop, and back up before attempting these exercises. Creating a safe learning environment allows you to be as confident and relaxed as possible around your horse. It also lessens the chances of your horse accidentally causing you injury.

> *We assume that you have specific knowledge of safety around horses or that you will always work through these exercises with an experienced horse person present.*

Awareness of your body space around your horse

The space around you that feels safe when you are with your horse or other people is referred to as your "body space bubble." It is up to you to decide where this is, and your horse is *only* allowed into your bubble if you permit this.

You can invite your horse into your space by taking up the slack on the lead rope so there is a slight "pressure" (without pulling them in), by drawing them in with your intention (i.e., creating a mental picture of them approaching you), or by moving closer and touching your horse.

Key points to remember:

- *If your horse moves towards you without your invitation, set a personal boundary with your body posture (stand firmly on the ground, keep your arms in front of you) or by gently holding a lunge or dressage whip in front of you to create a boundary. You can also back your horse up.* Whatever you decide, *your safety comes first.* In fact, you may want to seek out additional support to explore these options when you start working with your horse. This is one example where a mentor can be helpful for you.

- *Demonstrate confidence in your space and actively decide if your horse may enter this space.* This confidence will create a relationship of consistent mutual respect between you and your horse. It allows the horse to recognize you as the leader of the herd. Some people may equate having an assertive and consistent stance around horses to having healthy boundaries with people in their lives.

Approaching and touching a horse

Touch is a fairly intimate thing for a prey animal. This means you might have to stand and wait, or leave and do something else, until your horse seems comfortable with your touch. Notice the energy in your body and theirs. Knowing when you can touch a particular horse is an understanding that comes with time and experience. (Note that we use the term *energy* interchangeably with *nonverbal signals* that humans give during their interactions with horses.)

Sharing the Present

Maintaining your body space bubble with your horse

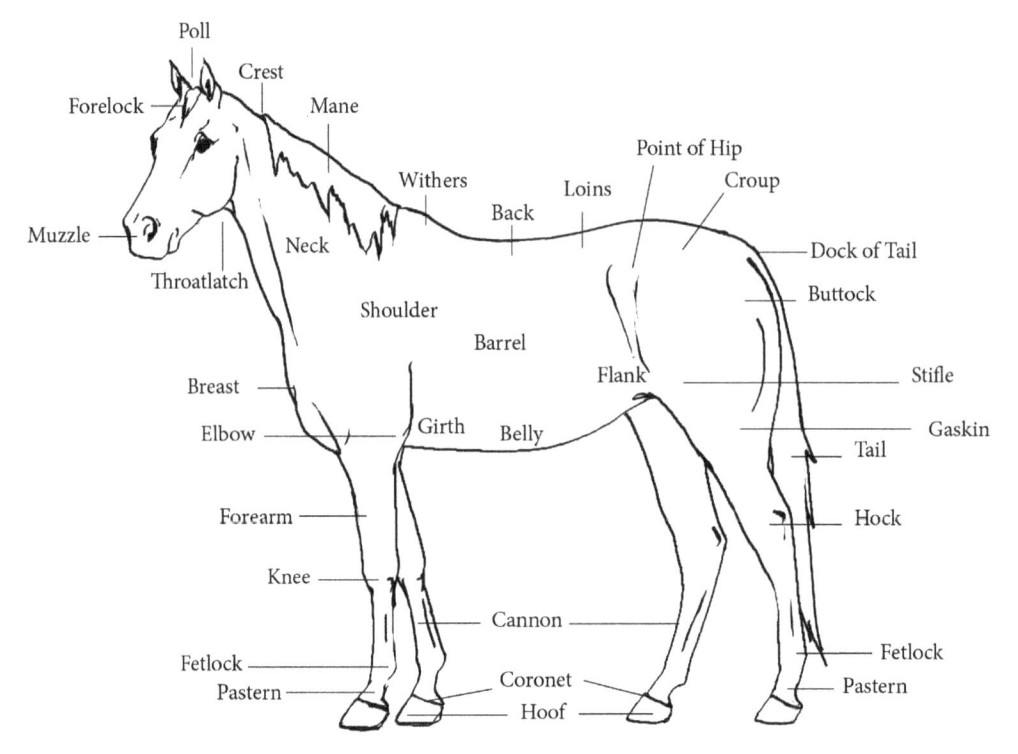

Touching a horse; areas of a horse's body

If you are unfamiliar with horses, approach a horse only with supervision. Here are other pointers that will help you to approach and interact with a horse:

- *When approaching a horse, always use your voice, sight, and touch.* Don't forget that you are approaching a prey animal that communicates nonverbally. They are built to be on alert for predators and can be highly reactive. This is why, when riding in a group, one horse may spook in reaction to an object and several other horses will also spook, without having seen the "spooky" object themselves.

- *Touch a horse first along its side, either at the shoulder, or at the neck just in front of the shoulder.* When standing near a horse, the safest position is between a horse's head and shoulder. Raising your hand, higher than the level of the withers, may make some horses tense—especially during initial contact. It is good to approach the horse at the side with your hand gently open or if approaching their muzzle, then with your palm closed in a fist (knuckles first). Do not approach a horse head on, with your arm outstretched, as this is a potentially threatening posture.

- *Consider the impact of providing a horse with treats.* We do not provide treats in these exercises as they can be distracting for both horse and human participants. However, this depends on whether you are already familiar with how your horse responds to treats and is left to your discretion.

- *Use appropriate footwear around a horse.* Use close-toed boots or shoes to avoid being injured if the horse accidentally steps on you.

- *Notice any signals that the horse feels threatened or uncomfortable.* These are described in the horse body language section later in this chapter. If you notice unease in your horse, take a few breaths and/or demonstrate calming signals (also explained later in this chapter). Then approach the horse again. Pause whenever you notice unease in your horse and repeat this process.

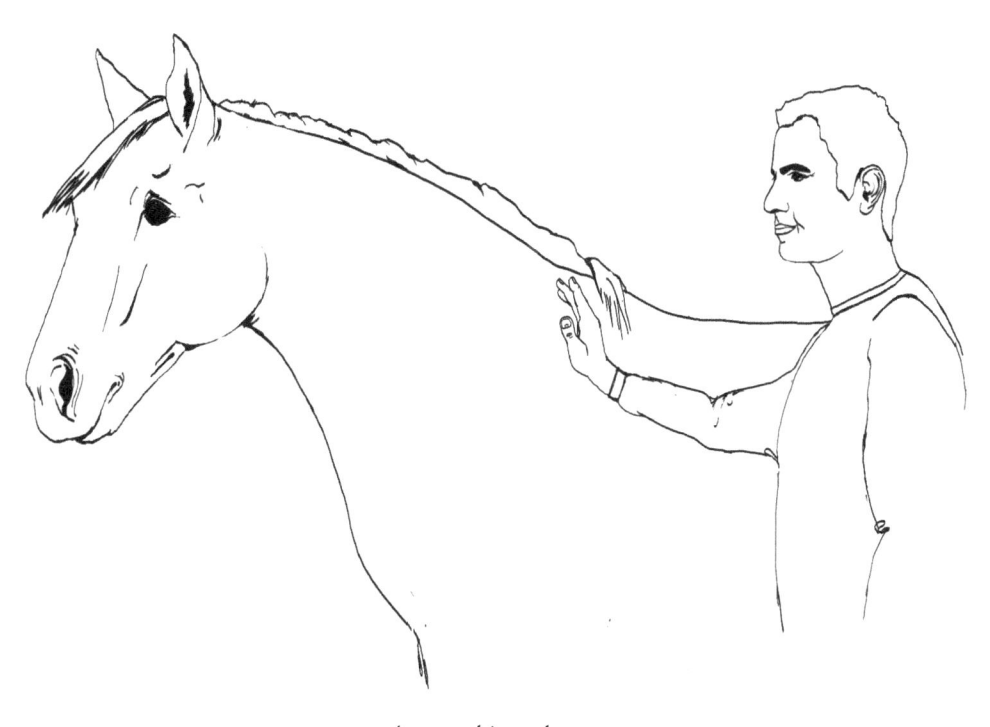

Approaching a horse

Sush approaching Stella, Next to Wild Photography

Walking around your horse

Give yourself enough safe space when walking around your horse. Here are a few recommendations:

- *Never place your face or head beneath a horse's head* when you are crossing from one side to the other. Always make sure you keep at least one full stride in front of the horse's muzzle. **Never** duck under the lead shank when your horse is tied, or crawl under the horse's belly or between their legs.

- *Be aware of the position of your head when near a horse's hooves.* Always remain on your feet and avoid kneeling when working with your horse's feet so that you can respond quickly and move away if the horse kicks out.

Sharing the Present

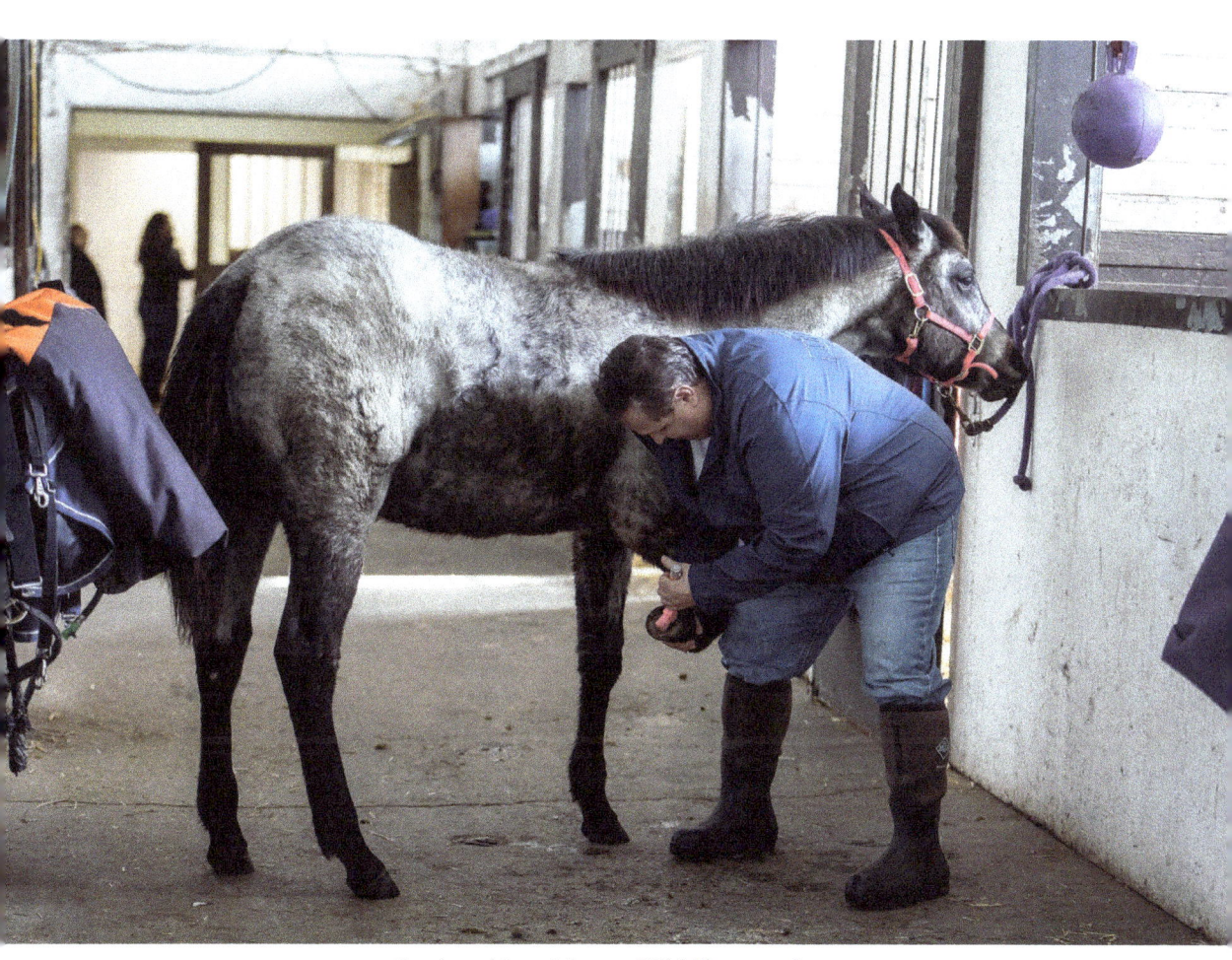

Frank and Jazz, Next to Wild Photography

Farrier Sheldon with Romeo, Next to Wild Photography

Sharing the Present

- *When moving behind a horse:*

    - *Walk at least one horse-length (about eight feet) behind a horse's rear.* This will help to keep you out of range of a potential kick.

    - *Alternatively, confidently walk right behind the horse, as close to the horse's rear as possible.* Let the horse know you are there using your touch and voice. This proximity minimizes the risk of injury from a possible kick. Aim to move smoothly rather than quickly, as sudden or quick movements can spook a horse.

- *Be aware of your position and the horse's position at all times.* Don't forget to maintain your body space bubble! The horse's hooves should not be so close to you that they can walk over your feet. If your horse is too close to you, push them firmly away. Respond immediately and consistently.

Awareness of horse and human body

Other safety suggestions

- *Consider wearing a helmet whenever you ride.* A properly fitted helmet will help reduce the risk of a brain injury should you fall or be thrown off.

The following activities are always best done with supervision until you are familiar with horses and the exercises:

- *Practise tying and untying a horse's lead rope.* When untying a horse, remember not to become trapped between the horse and a wall or fence.

- *Grooming.* Have a trusted mentor show you how to groom your horse in a way that is safe for you and comfortable for the horse.

- *Practise leading and riding a horse* until you are comfortable with the cues and aids for stopping a horse, backing them up, and moving them up or down through transitions. This suggestion applies before attempting Exercise 6 (Moving with your horse) and Exercise 7 (Riding mindfully).

> *What other ways help you to stay safe around your horse? What have you learned from others along the way about horse safety?*

Noticing general horse body language

Always pay attention to your horse's body language. This is both for the horse's physical and emotional well-being and for your own comfort. It is especially important while you are doing the exercises. Notice what your horse is telling you about whether they are comfortable or uncomfortable. Consider to what extent your horse's discomfort is affected by your emotional experiences and energy, remembering that horses are also capable of their own reactions, independent of you. The more you practise being aware of your horse's body language and reflecting on it, the better you will understand what your horse is communicating and why.

Sharing the Present

As you may know, horses communicate with people in diverse ways. Because they are non-verbal prey animals, horses have evolved to communicate their emotions through body position and movements of different part of their body. These include the position and movement of their ears and eyes, the set of their jaw, the degree of tension in their hindquarters and legs, and the movement of their tail, among other things. This section is just a brief overview of the subject, but there are many excellent resources on this topic (refer to Wilsie & Vogel, 2016, in our reference list at the end of this chapter).

What follows is not an exhaustive list, and any behavioural signs must be interpreted *within the larger context*. Remember that horses are individuals, so they will have their own idiosyncratic ways of communicating and their "normal" state of being. Thus, this list provides general tips only. For example, a sign such as chewing can mean different things depending on the bigger picture. As well, what is normal in one horse may be a sign of stress in another, depending on the unique personality of each.

Use these visual cues to help guide you when observing your horse's behaviours, as they are signs of their emotional state:

- *Calm or relaxed*—chewing motions, licking the lips, half-closed or fully closed eyes, a lowered head, a leg cocked and resting. Some horses will maintain eye contact, sigh, and position their ears slightly forwards.

- *Interest or curiosity*—an alert gaze and ears pricked forwards.

- *Disinterest*—the head or body turned away and the horse looking at other distractions in the environment.

- *Fear or anxiety*—wide prominent eyes, often showing the whites of the eyes, tense jaw, sudden stillness in the body, head raised and looking straight ahead, sudden movement.

- *Anger or dominance*—ears pinned back, threatening to bite, kicking movements, and swishing of the tail.

Shreyasi and Frank Brodhecker

Nervous horse

Sharing the Present

Fearful horse

Angry horse

Shreyasi and Frank Brodhecker

Panic in the paddock, Next to Wild Photography

Sharing the Present

Fearful horse, Next to Wild Photography

Anxious horse, Next to Wild Photography

Lonely horse, Next to Wild Photography

Sharing the Present

Peaceful Fiona, Prairie Darkroom Photography

Joy, Shay Rayann Photography

Horse calming signals

Research on calming signals was originally oriented to training with dogs, but was later extended to horses (Blake, 2015). These behaviours are a horse's way of signalling distress or being upset. Calling them "calming signals" is somewhat confusing, however, because they are *signs of stress*. More to the point, they are an animal's way of *calming themselves and others*—which sometimes includes the people around them—when the animal experiences stress or notices it in others.

It is useful to know that you can positively influence such moments and help to calm yourself and your horse by intentionally replicating some of these calming signals—such as yawning, blinking slowly, or softening your eyes (see details in the list below). This helps to reassure your horse. **Remember that if a horse is behaving dangerously during the mindfulness exercises, even if driven by stress, prioritize the safety rules ahead of implementing the calming signals.**

> *Calming signals are signs of stress. They are how animals calm themselves and others.*

Calming signals mimic what happens in a herd when one horse notices a threat and another notices that all is safe again—by communicating this message to the rest of the herd via certain behaviours that calm them all. By deliberately mimicking these calming behaviours, you assume a leadership role and communicate to the horse that all is safe, and they can relax. Showing calming signals when your horse feels threatened or nervous helps to defuse their alarm and reinforce your leadership position. Calming signals are also part of displaying non-threatening body language in your initial approach to a horse.

Please remember to look at the "bigger picture." If you notice your horse displaying these calming signals pay attention to what the rest of your horse is doing. Do they appear tense or relaxed? Are they pacing? Swishing their tail? Stomping? Is something else happening simultaneously? The bigger picture often involves more than just what is happening with your horse—it usually means there is something else happening in the environment, with other horses, people, and so forth.

Inspired by the quote below, we invite you to reflect on the parallels between exploring horses' behaviour and children's behaviour (try replacing the word "children" with "horses" as you read this quote):

> *Children don't need to be fixed because they aren't broken. Often what needs to change are our own expectations and ideas about how our children should be. Children have a better chance of reaching their full potential when they are part of a system that focuses on children's needs rather than their behaviour and performance (Samson, 2019).*

Look for calming signals like these:

- *In the eyes.* A relaxed horse has a soft, calm look in the eye and typically blinks about once every ten seconds. The eye appears soft and round, with possibly a round wrinkle (that is, an inverted U-shaped deep fold) above the eyelid. With increasing stress, the following two calming signals may be noted (in order of increasing intensity):

    - A triangle or diamond-like shape in the upper eyelid. More wrinkles are evident above the upper eyelid and blinking increases to one blink per second.

    - A triangle shape in the upper eyelids. Multiple wrinkles appear above the eyelid, the whites of the eyes show, and the horse blinks one or more times per second.

- *In the ears.* Horses' ears are very mobile, so simply watching the ears is insufficient to assess whether a horse is relaxed. When stress is rising, the horse's ears may quickly move forward and back. Ears that are tightly turned back or pinned can mean that the stress level is increasing or that the horse is becoming angry or aggressive.

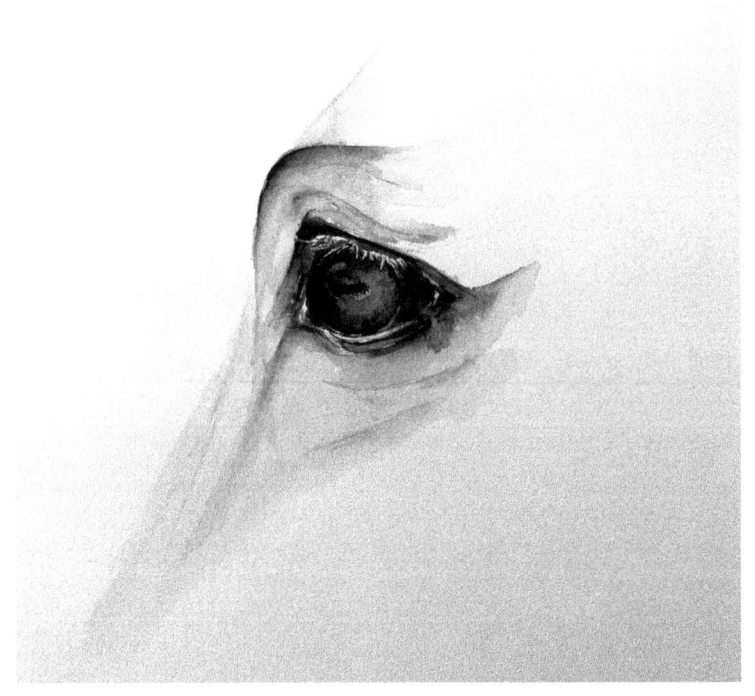

Wrinkles appearing, mild stress state

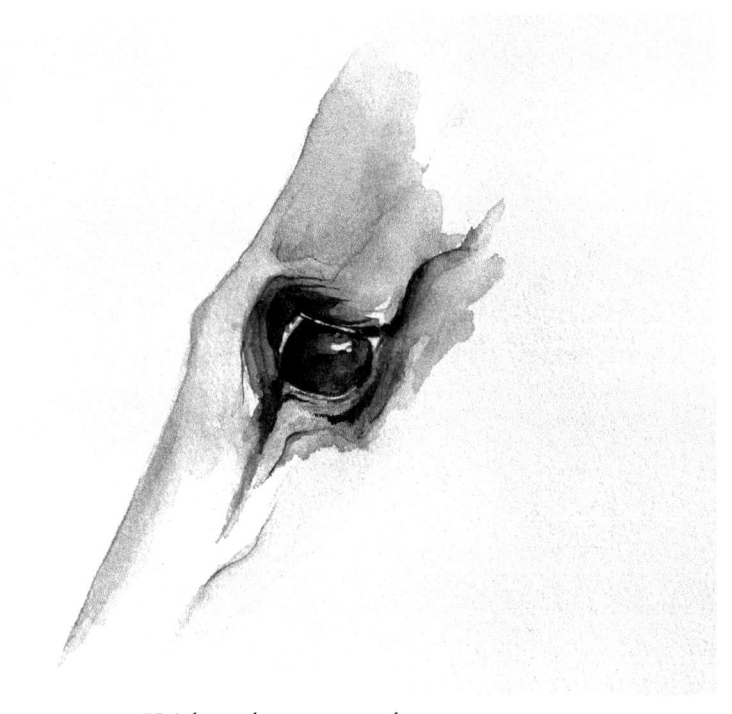

Heightened stress or moderate stress state

Sharing the Present

Extreme stress state

- *In the tail.* When a horse is relaxed, the tail tends to hang loosely and may swing in the rhythm of the horse's steps. As a horse becomes progressively more stressed, the following two calming signals may occur (in order of increasing intensity):

    - Tail tucked in between the buttocks. Swishing the tail may be a sign of growing irritation and tension.

    - Tail lifted like a flag to suggest excitement and tension or that the horse is considering flight—running away from the situation they are in.

  For those readers who are new to horses, note that horses also lift their tail before passing urine or having a bowel movement.

Calming signals in the horse body

Calming a stressed horse

Signs that indicate a horse may be under stress (these overlap with the descriptions of fear and dominance above) are the following:

- *Ready for flight.* Tail lifted, head raised, shoulders tense, positioned with body weight disproportionately placed on front legs (as if ready to push off from their hindquarters), sudden stillness in the body; nostrils may be flared.

- *Engaging in behaviours like licking and chewing.* Suggests high stress levels instead of calm depending on context. Of course, placing this in the larger context is important so that you know what the licking and chewing means; that is, whether the horse is stressed or calm.

- *Freezing.* Standing very still

- *"Fight" response.* Ears pinned back, attempts to bite, kicking movements, and rapid swishing of the tail.

> *Reflect on how your horse shows you that they are calm. Considering this, how can you detect stress in your horse?*

It is important to note that horses rarely demonstrate their initial discomfort through large displays of stress. In fact, most horses will display their discomfort in very subtle ways to begin with. Differences in the individual horse's temperament and sensitivity also affect how they express their distress, as do breed-specific differences. Knowing the specific horse you are working with helps you understand what their "normal" is and to identify when something changes. Stay as observant as possible, watching your horse closely during the exercises for these subtle signs: slowing down in their movements, stopping blinking, or blinking at a very rapid rate. Always interpret these signs in the context of the horse's situation, so you can avoid jumping to inaccurate conclusions.

Some specific strategies and pointers for calming your horse:

- *Your safety comes first.* Never compromise your safety in a dangerous situation. If you feel you are in any danger, with the help of an experienced horse person, intervene to re-establish your safety and then re-evaluate the situation. If no experienced horse person is present and you feel in danger, then you should remove yourself from the situation.

- *Pay immediate and close attention when your horse is stressed during an exercise.* They may show this by conveying fear or anger. If you missed your horse's initial stress cues, the calming strategies may still be useful. What is your horse "saying" to you? What were you doing when this behaviour first appeared? What can you do to settle the horse?

- *Talk to your horse in a calm, soft voice, blinking slowly, yawning, and stroking the withers.* Purposefully relax your own body. These actions together show leadership and communicate that you are sensitive to your horse's distress.

- *Help your horse to disengage from what they were focused on by moving their feet.* Regardless of whether you are riding or on the ground, you can achieve this by leading them in circles, backing them up, or engaging in lateral work. Note that some horses benefit from being invited to remain still if they have been pacing back and forth in anxiety. If you need practise moving your horse's feet, work on this skill with an experienced horse person or instructor before participating in any of the exercises.

- *Use calming strategies BEFORE the horse's stress escalates.* The optimal time to calm your horse is before they get to the point when they exhibit large displays of stress (R. Bignell, personal communication, March 21, 2019). In such a scenario, you can mindfully notice that the horse is showing subtle signals of distress and then intervene using some of the calming strategies listed.

- *Select activities that your horse is comfortable with and has had previous success completing.* When free to move in this way, it creates an opportunity for the horse to naturally release tension and reduce levels of stress. Horses feel this stress through physiological arousal that includes elevated levels of cortisol and adrenaline. Familiar movements lessen this state of physiological arousal by allowing the natural de-stressing process to occur.

> *If you have some experience, reflect on other ways that have worked to calm your horse in the past. Feel free to use these approaches during the mindfulness exercises, if necessary.*

Summary

If you are new to horses and feel unsafe with your horse, dismount and back away. If you are being supervised, follow the guidance being given to you. We recognize that experienced riders may persist in certain situations. Since we cannot predict how each exercise will feel for every horse and equestrian, remember to always follow the safety rules—as you would with any equine activity. The risks are never completely eliminated but remaining attentive to these rules will go a long way to keeping you and your horse safe.

Now that we have discussed some ideas about how to take care of yourself and your horse through these exercises, take some deep breaths in and out. Relax! We reviewed these strategies so that you can be comfortable and prepared, and we expect that this will be an enjoyable learning process for you AND your horse. Combining mindfulness with horses is a wonderful and rewarding way to learn a new skill and to develop a relationship with your equine partner. We are excited for you to start the journey!

Shreyasi and Frank Brodhecker

Trust

References and resources

Sources cited

Blake, A. (2015). "Horse's Calming Signals in Practice." https://one-horselife.com/horses-calming-signals-in-practice-3

Equestrian Canada. *Western Rider Handbook, levels 1–4.* (2017). Ottawa, ON: Equestrian Canada.

Samson, R. [@sensitivityproject]. (2019, February 14). Children don't need to be fixed because they aren't broken. https://www.instagram.com/p/Bt3KbEfnZbR

Siegel, D. (1999). *The Developing Mind: How Relationships and the Brain Interact to Shape Who We Are.* New York, NY: Guilford Publications.

Wilsie, S., & Vogel, G. (2016). *Horse Speak: An Equine-Human Translation Guide.* North Pomfret, VT: Trafalgar Square Press.

Other resources

Schoning, B., & Grutzner, H. (2016). *Horse Behaviour: Interpreting Body Language and Communication.* Sheffield, UK: 5M Publishing.

Websites (Sue McIntosh)

https://healinghooves.ca/life-lessons-from-a-border-collie-e-motion-needs-to-move

https://healinghooves.ca/why-horses-animals-and-psychoeducation https://healinghooves.ca/is-no-fear-a-good-thing

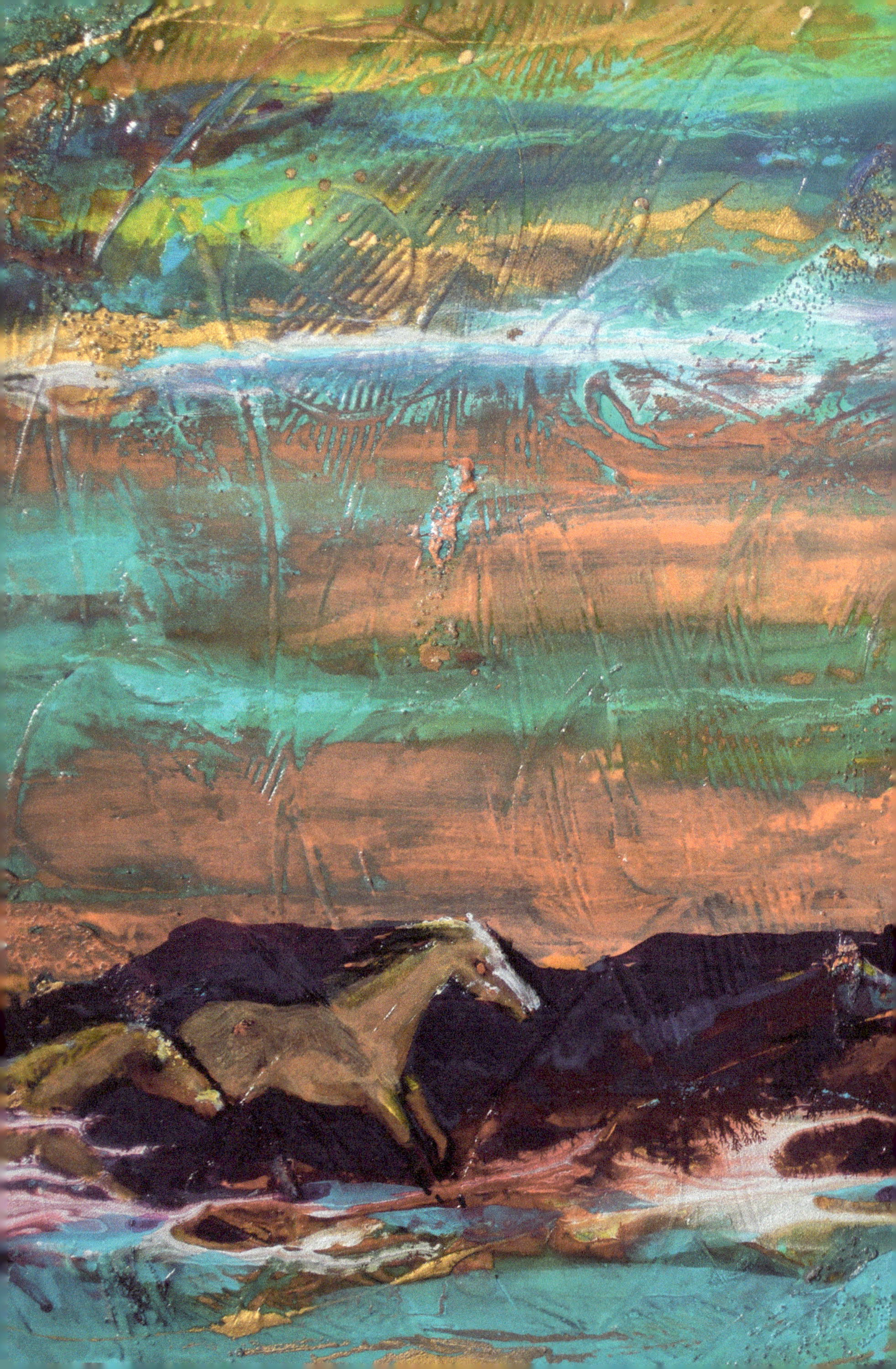

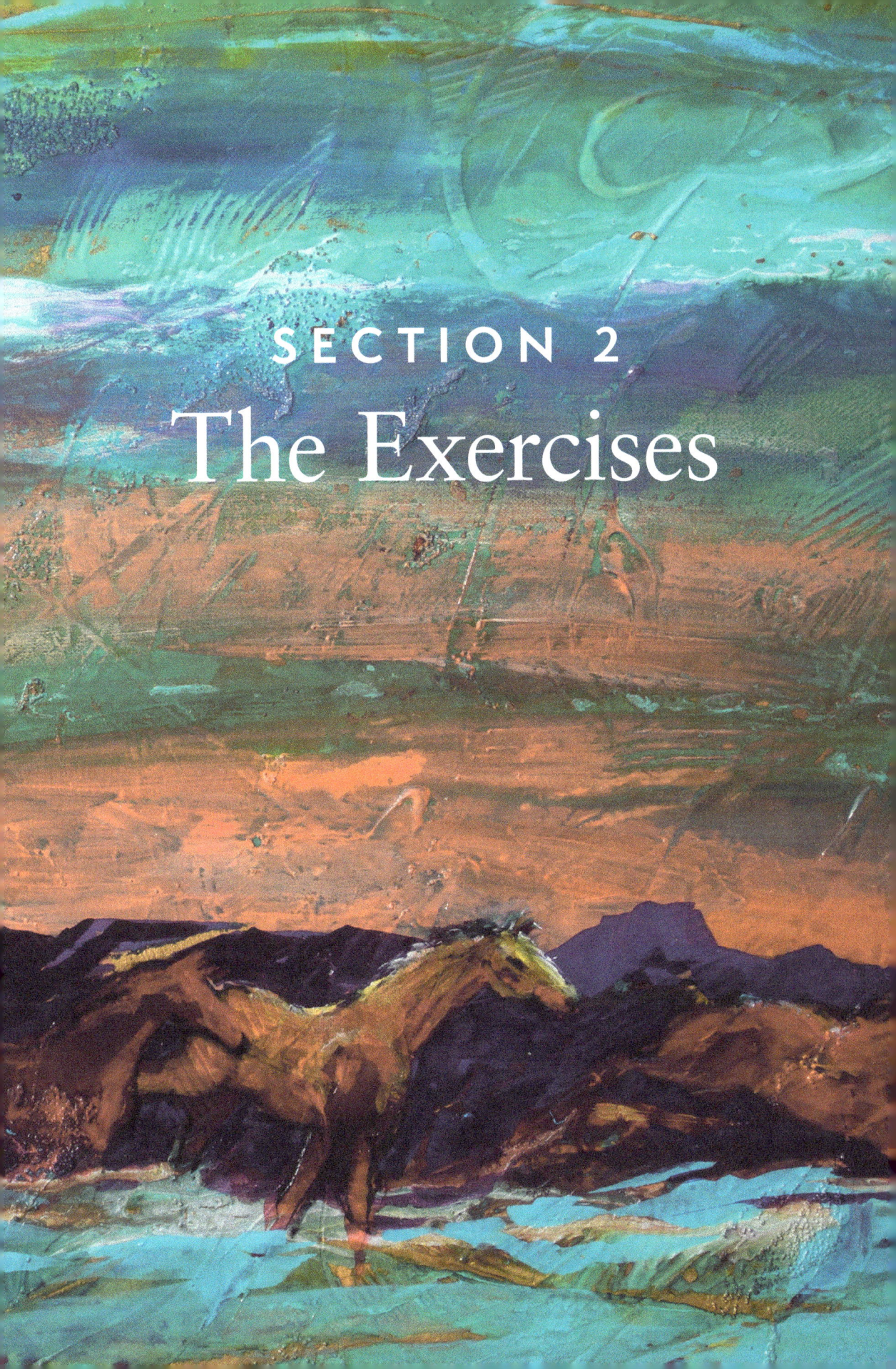

SECTION 2
The Exercises

Braxton and Violet sharing a quiet moment, SJ Originals Photography

CHAPTER 4

Introducing the Interactive Exercises

In the vessel of your body, you yourself are the world tree, deep roots in the Earth and a crown of stars. Your essence bridges dimensions.

~~ Elizabeth Eiler

This section presents the mindfulness exercises, which are designed to improve your connection with your horse. Each exercise has three parts: an introduction, guidance for the activity, and suggested modifications. Videos and guided audio files of the exercises are also provided at www.mindfulmarewellness.com so that you can access what is most useful for you.

The exercises are designed to be practised in three different contexts:

1. *On your own*—away from your horse.

2. *Across the fence*—while your horse is in a paddock, pasture, or stall. These exercises allow space for you to practise the mindfulness skills without distraction.

3. *With your horse*—in the same area, but either a distance away or right next to your horse, depending on what is specified in the exercise. You could be with your horse in the paddock, pasture, arena, or elsewhere.

Horse kisses, Megan Kruse Photography

Greeting, Shay Rayann Photography

Some exercises start with the first context and evolve into ones you can practise in your horse's presence (whether nearby or farther away) as your mindfulness skills strengthen.

All the exercises are influenced by those we have encountered in the Mindfulness-Based Stress Reduction program, within the mindfulness module of Dialectical Behavior Therapy and the mindfulness literature of Thich Nhat Hanh (see the resources section of Chapter 1). The exercises have been modified based on our personal experiences with our horses. We are not specifically horse experts or mindfulness experts; we bring experience from both worlds.

The equestrian skills and orientations influencing these exercises are from our understanding of Centered Riding®, Connected Riding®, and Tellington *TTouch*® approaches. We also build on groundwork and riding instruction that uses pressure and release techniques, which we have learned from some of our own instructors. We are continually learning, and we offer these exercises based on our *current* levels of mindfulness and equestrian experience, as well as our personal experience of practising the exercises with our own horses.

The exercises are intentionally sequenced so that your mindfulness skills can deepen over time (although there is no striving to get anywhere). Although unlikely, if there are times when you or your horse experience stress during the exercises, please use the strategies reviewed in Chapter 3 of Section 1. There may be occasions when you decide that certain exercises are not suitable for you and/or your horse. In such cases, feel free to move on to the other exercises.

Most of the exercise guides include questions to reflect on after you have completed the exercise. Part of practising mindfulness is being able to explore what happened for you during practice, which enriches the process of paying attention in this way. The reflection points after each exercise help you explore this. We also include blank pages at the end of the book for reflection space.

Finally, you may notice that the language used is simple and invitational. Some exercises contain phases to cue you to notice yourself, your horse, and then both of you at the same time. However, these labels ("phase 1", "phase 2") can be ignored if you find that they are interfering with a coherent experience of the exercises. The language is phrased as if we are there guiding you, so there are several "ing" words (i.e., the present participle), such as "observing", "feeling", "walking", etc., since these are direct parts of your experience in the exercises. This may take some getting used to. Watching the video or playing the guided audio file for an exercise, available at www.mindfulmarewellness.com, may enrich your experience as well.

It is completely natural to be distracted during the exercises. As mentioned before, if you notice your mind is focused on something else, notice and bring attention back to the chosen focus of the exercise. The sensations, thoughts, and emotions that distracted you may still be there, but your attention is directed to the exercise.

People often ask how long these exercises will take. The short answer is that it depends. When you first try these exercises, you may notice moving more slowly than usual. With practice you can adjust the exercises to any time, pace, and place with your horse. Start by setting aside at least 15 minutes for an exercise and adjust accordingly. Depending on how an exercise goes for you that day, you may choose for it to be slower or faster, according to your preference. You can also repeat the same exercise on several occasions, as many times as you like. This is *your* journey of discovery, and *you* are the expert on what you need from this book.

Overview of the exercises

We begin with the *Foundation Exercise*—so-named because it is the background against which all the other exercises take place. This initial exercise invites you to ground yourself and is an exercise you can use to start your mindfulness practice outside of the barn.

The remaining exercises are grouped and categorized to help build your mindfulness skills.

Sensory awareness

Exercises 1 and 2 focus on being present with your horse by accessing the senses of sight, touch, and smell, along with the rhythm of breathing.

- Exercise #1: Watching—Truly seeing your horse

- Exercise #2: Breathing and being with your horse

Equestrian skills awareness

This section builds physical awareness of your bodily movements and those of your horse when they are in motion, through walking, leading, and riding body awareness exercises. Exercises 3 through 6 are suitable for those with any level of horse experience, provided there is access to an equine instructor or coach. Exercise 7 is intended for riders of all experience levels.

- Exercise #3: Body awareness near your horse
- Exercise #4: Touch and connection
- Exercise #5: Grooming your horse mindfully
- Exercise #6: Moving with your horse (applicable to groundwork or just walking with your horse)
- Exercise #7: Riding mindfully—Being one with your horse while riding

Cognitive and emotional awareness

Exercise 8 is designed to help you practise being aware of your thoughts and emotions when you are with your horse.

- Exercise #8: Awareness of thoughts and emotions—Expectations, judgments, and feelings

Relationship awareness

Exercises 9 and 10 allow you to explore the relationship with your horse.

- Exercise #9: Being thankful for your horse
- Exercise #10: Letting go

> 🐎 *You can "anchor" yourself in the present by noticing the following:*
>
> 1. Your five senses (sensory awareness)
> 2. Your physical sensations (body awareness)
> 3. Your emotions and thoughts (internal emotional and cognitive awareness)
> 4. Your connection to your horse (relationship awareness)
> 5. Your horse's body language (awareness of others)
>
> You can use these anchors when you are alone or when you are with others.

Putting it all together

Most of these exercises support staying mindful by focusing on one thing at a time. However, some mindfulness approaches also encourage practitioners to notice several things at once. Exercise 11 reflects this view, which you can pursue after completing the earlier exercises, or when you feel ready. Exercise 12 concludes with a list of additional ideas for brief, everyday mindfulness exercises that you might adapt for use in your everyday life.

We conclude rather than start with these briefer exercises in Exercise 12, as we hope that having reached that point in the book, you will have a stronger understanding and practice of mindfulness skills. You will, therefore, be better able to fall into a mindful state of being for brief moments of time.

- Exercise #11: Putting it all together
- Exercise #12: Other ways to be mindful around your horse

> 🐎 *The various exercises are designed to be flexible to your comfort and needs. You can build your mindfulness skills in many ways while staying true to yourself and honouring your horse's comfort.*

Summary

This overview introduces the mindfulness practices that will be expanded upon in the rest of this book. The exercises help you to explore mindfulness during time spent with your horse. We hope that these exercises will be a start to a lifelong mindfulness practice—informally with horses, and formally through other mindfulness learning of your choosing.

Grace's hoofbeats, SJ Originals Photography

CHAPTER 5
Mindfulness Exercises

Foundation Exercise: Grounding

Intro

This exercise is to be practised before approaching your horse.

Context

On your own (entirely away from your horse); *across the fence* while your horse is in the pasture or paddock. This gives your horse the space and freedom to move away if they prefer.

The exercise invites you to notice yourself right now—your body, breathing sensations, your mind (thoughts and emotions), and your focus or concentration. This allows release of emotional and physical tension before you spend time with your horse and to tune in to your horse's safety and your own. Note that we'll include some version of this grounding exercise in the first part of each exercise instruction. With practice, you can apply this exercise at any time of the day, to recalibrate your mindfulness compass or to tune into the present moment.

Since you are practising mindfulness for the first time in this way, we have suggested starting at a distance from your horse. Practising at a distance from your horse allows you to explore your feelings when first trying this without keeping track of what your horse is doing at the same time. This also allows you to practise without having expectations of the horse's behaviours during the exercise.

It is natural for your mind to occasionally be occupied with other things or for your attention to shift while reading the guidance. We invite you to keep an open mind and notice your experience. You can include quiet moments in this exercise if you choose. You can also listen to the audio file or watch the video for this exercise at www.mindfulmarewellness.com to see what it is like.

You may like or dislike certain exercises depending on the day, and either is fine because the key is just to notice what happens. You may find that you do better if you have someone read the words to you or listening to the audio file as you practice.

As you practise the exercise, keep track of when a body sensation or thought or emotion becomes overwhelming. Refer to the strategies in Chapter 3 to help you stay within your window of tolerance and feel safe. You can explore these things later with a friend or mental health professional if you want.

After the guidance, we include another option to achieve calm energy before approaching your horse. We explain soft eyes in detail in Exercise 1 of this section. For now, just think of it as a relaxed gaze.

Guidance

Begin with noticing the *state of your body*—whether your body feels relaxed, in pain, fatigued, or something else. Now focus attention on physical sensations presenting in certain body parts. Hold attention in these areas, while curiously noting the quality of these sensations. There may be tingling, heaviness, lightness, or other qualities showing up. Invite yourself to feel this information without changing it in any way. Sensations in the body naturally shift over time; track these changes as best you can.

If certain sensations in the body are overwhelming, take care of yourself through the moment by adjusting your body position, stretching, massaging a sore area, or focusing on another part of the body that feels comfortable. Tending to yourself is part of the process.

Check in now with the *five senses*. Note what you are *seeing* and *hearing* in the surroundings. Register any *smells* or *tastes* arising. Feel your body *touching* certain surfaces, such as your feet on the ground or clothing against your skin. As best you can, allow whatever you notice to be the way it is, without trying to change it. Recognizing whether your attention has shifted elsewhere is part of this practice; if this happens, note where the attention lies before gently returning it back to the five senses.

Taking a deep breath in and out, in the next moment, shift attention to a part of the body where you easily notice the sensations of *breathing*. This might be in your nostrils, in your stomach, or in your chest as it rises and falls with your breath, or it may be somewhere else. Patiently noticing the sensations of breathing at a natural pace from one moment to the next.

Now tune in to your *state of mind*, consciously detecting thoughts or emotions that may be present. At each moment, choosing to hold the thoughts or emotions in the field of attention or stepping away from them if you are overwhelmed. You can breathe through overwhelming thoughts or emotions or place them in an imaginary container, to which you can return later. If your body needs some care, then make gentle adjustments such as shifting position or stretching.

Reflect now on how *focused you are* in this moment. Rather than forcing yourself to concentrate in a certain way, simply notice if your attention shifts rapidly or remains placed on one aspect of the present moment experience. With the next exhale, let go of this exercise.

Congratulations, you have just practised your first mindfulness exercise!

Achieving calm energy near your horse

1. Taking three *deep breaths*
2. Relaxing your gaze as you look at the surroundings and your horse, practising *soft eyes*
3. Setting an *intention to connect* with your horse
4. Approaching your horse after you start feeling a *calm energy*

Treasure's soft eyes, Amanda Ubell Photography

Sharing the Present

Exercise #1: Watching— Truly seeing your horse

Watching your horse

Watching your horse (2)

Shreyasi and Frank Brodhecker

Violet's gaze, Amanda Ubell Photography

Sharing the Present

The herd at sunset, Amanda Ubell Photography

Intro

This exercise is a gentle reminder to *notice* all there is to see when you watch your horse.

Context

First, across the fence; later, with your horse

People naturally look at horses most of the time that they are with them—in a stall or pasture, during grooming and tacking up, and when working in the arena, round pen, or out in the open. In this exercise, we invite you to look at your horse in a completely different way—looking at them with a mindful way of noticing.

When you see your horse this way, you practise seeing them with attitudes of *non-judgment* and *beginner's mind*. Your horse is not entirely the same day-to-day, or even from one moment to the next, just as is the case with us. When you practise noticing them without letting expectations influence what you see, you notice things more accurately in the present moment. This is the start of bringing mindful awareness to time spent with your horse.

This across-the-fence exercise—while the horse is freely moving in a pasture, paddock, or stall—allows both you and your horse to feel comfortable, regardless of your level of experience. The idea is to try a new way of watching your horse, and this is easier to do when you are at a distance. By practising this way, you also have the space to deal with unexpected feelings or thoughts without being distracted by your horse.

If your horse seems stressed, based on body language, you can try the calming strategies we discussed. Examples are blinking slowly, taking deep breaths in and out to relax, or looking away and then back at your horse. You can also try talking to your horse softly and/or stroking the withers. If your horse approaches you and you would like to touch them briefly, that is completely fine provided you can then take a few steps away to continue with mindful seeing.

This exercise relies on a concept from Centered Riding® called "soft eyes," first developed by Sally Swift. You practise soft eyes when you look at an object in its environment, while intentionally relaxing your facial expressions and reducing the intensity of your stare. People often invest a good deal of energy to concentrate on specific things in front of them, looking at them with a hard gaze or intent stare (hard eyes). Sometimes, when you *think* intently about something, you also look with hard eyes. Horses feel more comfortable when you watch them with soft eyes. Using soft eyes reduces your tension and helps you adopt a calm state of being/energy around your horse.

> *Practise SOFT EYES*
>
> - Intentionally relax your gaze
>
> - Expand your visual awareness to include the peripheral vision and surroundings
>
> - Enhance your physical awareness of soft eyes by reflecting on how it feels in your facial muscles, as well as your breathing. Notice the difference in the sensations when using soft eyes vs. hard eyes.
>
> - Remember that soft eyes are the *opposite* of intent staring.

Shreyasi and Frank Brodhecker

Lucky, SJ Originals Photography

Joe's soft eyes, SJ Originals Photography

Shreyasi and Frank Brodhecker

Honey, SJ Originals Photography

Guidance

Phase 1: Take a few moments to observe how your body feels, now choosing a point where you can stand and watch your horse. Feel your feet resting on the ground. Tune into breathing sensations where they feel most apparent—either in the nostrils, the chest, or abdomen—feeling the expanding and contracting. Pay close attention to the physical sensations of breathing, allowing your eyes to be softly closed or resting half closed as you focus on a point on the ground in front of you.

Intentionally raise your gaze, practising soft eyes and noticing the entire breadth of your surroundings. Let the details of the environment glide onto your field of vision without seeking or scanning. Taking in the periphery with soft eyes. Consciously place your gaze on your horse, noticing whether your horse is looking at you or elsewhere. Noticing if they are moving or standing still. Paying attention to their body language such as the position of the ears, head, and tail. Noticing signs of relaxation, inquisitiveness, restlessness, or something else in your horse.

As you continue watching, take in aspects of your horse's physical appearance. Notice changes in light or dark surfaces, coat colour and appearance, symmetry, or asymmetry, whatever else there is to see. Take your time, intentionally shifting your gaze across specific body parts such as the face and muzzle, the neck and shoulders, the withers, back and girth, the legs and tail. Simply allowing the eyes to fully take in your horse's appearance, registering sensory details without altering them in any way. There may be feelings or thoughts arising, including evaluations of your horse's conformation, breed, age, or something else. If attention shifts in this way, let the feelings and thoughts remain in the background while mindfully seeing your horse.

At this time, tune in to any physical sensations, curiously exploring your body's reaction as you watch your horse. Know that you can take care of yourself if you are emotionally or physically overwhelmed by feeling breath sensations in the body, massaging a sore area, or adjusting your position.

Phase 2: Taking care of your horse is also part of this practice. If they show signs of unease, try practising soft eyes, taking deep breaths, or briefly looking elsewhere and then back at them. If it is available, bring appreciation to your soft eyes.

Intentionally shift the gaze away from your horse and then, returning it back, observe the effect on their body language and in your body, continuing to stand and witness what they are offering. Simply be with them by watching in this way. Allow your gaze to widen again to pay visual attention to the entire landscape. On the next exhale, let go of the exercise.

Reflecting after the Exercise

- *What did you notice in this exercise?* This may include reactions of comfort or discomfort, evaluations of the exercise, physical sensations or emotions arising for you, your impressions of your horse, or something else.

- *How is this way of seeing different than your usual approach with your horse?* Note the differences from the usual way of watching your horse. Note whether you liked seeing them this way, or if it was confusing and frustrating. You may have a different experience every time you try this exercise.

- *What do you think this exercise was like for your horse?* We encourage you to reflect on details observed in your horse's body language. Notice if this changes each time you practise the exercise.

- *How does this exercise affect how you feel about your horse, if at all? How might this way of watching your horse be helpful?*

Modifications

After sufficient practice and when you think you are ready to handle unexpected feelings or thoughts, try this:

- *Watch your horse at a closer distance.* You may want someone who is more experienced with horses to be with you during the exercise.

- *Practise walking around your horse or moving closer or farther away from them.* This adds the element of movement, while still watching your horse and paying attention in a patient and open way. When approaching your horse, intentionally slow your breathing, blink slowly, practise soft eyes, and adopt a calm energy.

- *Watching a herd.* If your horse shares a pasture or paddock with other horses, you can practice widening and narrowing the gaze and maintaining soft eyes to explore a specific horse, or the herd and their interactions/behaviours, visually.

This exercise may also be useful with difficult-to-catch horses. Watching them mindfully, and possibly haltering and then un-haltering them right after, may make a difference in their willingness to be haltered.

A quick note: If this is the first exercise you have tried with your horse, give yourself a pat on the back! You have already made a step forward in terms of understanding your horse's way of paying attention to the world and in training your mind to be attentive to the present. Feel free to journal or discuss some of your observations with trusted others. The more you practise describing what you observe using simple factual language, the easier it becomes to notice what's happening in the present moment.

Shreyasi and Frank Brodhecker

Exercise #2: Breathing and being with your horse

Breathing with your horse

Sharing the Present

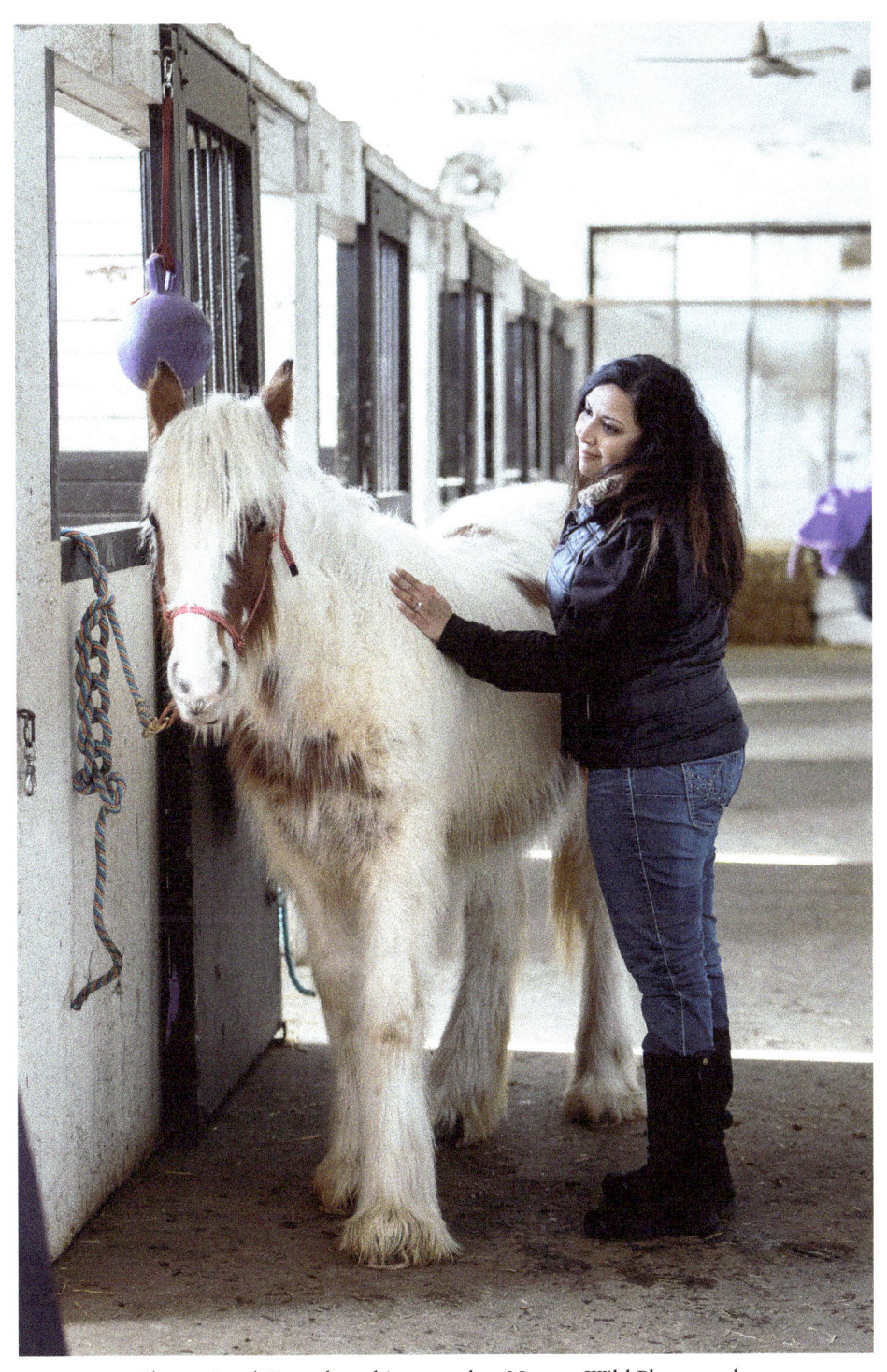

Shreyasi and Grace breathing together, Next to Wild Photography

Desiree breathing with her horse, Megan Kruse Photography

Braxton and Violet, SJ Originals Photography

Intro

This exercise is an effective way to immediately feel connected to your body and relate to your horse in the present moment, especially when you are stuck inside your thoughts.

Context

First, *across the fence* and then *with* your *horse*

This is the first exercise in the book where you are invited to notice a body connection between you and your horse; in this case, through the sensation of breathing. The other exercises in the book build on the physical resonance between you and your horse in other ways. As you practise this exercise, you intentionally notice you and your horse breathing together (although at different rates).

A horse's rib cage rises and falls as they inhale and exhale, and they breathe at a slower rate than humans do. Observing their belly or flanks over time may help you recognize these movements. Occasionally, people can see slight movement at the base of the horse's nostrils.

Although this is initially practised across the fence, how far you are from your horse depends on the distance needed to observe physical signs of breathing patterns. If you are across the fence and your horse moves away from you, just do your best.

If you are with your horse, you may practise soft eyes and take a couple of steps towards your horse, if that helps you observe the breathing more easily. This is usually possible if you have some horse experience or a comfortable relationship with the horse you are partnering with for this exercise. If your horse remains standing still, then continue the exercise from this closer vantage point. However, if the horse moves away after you've taken a couple of steps towards them, maintain this distance during the exercise. Notice whether you have thoughts or judgments about this as you complete the exercise. If your horse approaches, you may touch them briefly before resuming the exercise in a mindful way.

If your horse appears stressed, practise the calming signals we described in Chapter 3 of Section One and notice their response. If this does not help, consider stopping the exercise and doing something enjoyable with your horse such as grooming or letting them graze.

> *Notice the fluidity of the movements between you and your horse, resembling a dance.*

Why would you be invited to observe your horse's breathing? This exercise links to the HeartMath research described in Chapter 1 of Section One. That research revealed that horses have large electromagnetic fields around their hearts, relative to other animals. When people are in the presence of such energy, it may affect their own electromagnetic energy fields; this could be one reason why some people feel such a sense of peace and calm around horses (Gehrke, 2013). Observe your emotional state during this exercise, and how it shifts over time. This is an opportunity to notice how you and your horse influence each other, even when you are doing something as simple as standing near each other.

The key reminder of this exercise is that your breath is always there with you to bring focus on to the present moment. The intent is to stay mindful of how you influence each other, rather than matching your breathing patterns to those of your horse. (Most horses breathe more slowly than people do, making it uncomfortable to mimic their exact breathing rates.) Breathing in through your nose and out through your mouth instead may affect your horse's breathing so that they respond by sighing or relaxing in other ways. You can experiment with these shifts in your breathing and observe how your horse responds in each moment. As with other exercises, you can read the text, ask someone to read to you, listen to the audio file for this exercise or watch the video prior to attempting it yourself.

Guidance

Phase 1: Start by paying attention to your body, and then briefly tune in to thoughts and emotions and to how focused your attention is in this moment. Settle your feet on the ground, feeling anchored to the earth. Welcome breathing at a natural rhythm, breathing as lightly or deeply as feels comfortable, bringing your primary focus of attention to the sensations of your breath. Attend to these sensations in the entire body or in a part of the body where it is easiest to track. Breathing sensations may be obvious in the nostrils or throat, the chest rising and falling, or perhaps the abdomen expanding and contracting with each breath.

Phase 2: Holding a soft-eyed gaze and a gentle heart, intentionally approach your horse, welcoming them silently, however you choose. Notice your horse moving away or closer to you as you slowly approach. As you reach a position across the fence or closer, depending on your choice for this exercise, continue breathing mindfully. Notice that your horse is breathing, watching their nostrils, rib cage, belly, or flank. Pay close attention to their breathing while expanding attention to also notice your breathing. Rest in this special awareness of the two of you breathing together. Allow thoughts and emotions that make themselves known to reside in the background, while your bodies breathing together becomes the primary focus of your attention.

As you continue breathing, notice the space between you and your horse and the physical and emotional connection of breathing together. On the next exhale, release this exercise.

Reflecting after the Exercise

- *What did you notice in this exercise?* This may include reactions of comfort or discomfort, evaluations of the exercise, physical sensations or emotions arising for you, your impressions of your horse, or something else.

- *How is this way of being with your horse different than the usual approach with your horse?* Note the differences. Also notice whether you liked this way of being with them, or if it was confusing and frustrating. You may have a different experience every time you try this exercise.

- *What do you think this exercise was like for your horse?* We encourage you to reflect on the details you observed in your horse's body language. Notice if this changes each time you practise the exercise.

- *How does this exercise affect how you feel about your horse, if at all? How might this way of being with your horse be helpful?*

> *Can you see yourself noticing your breathing in this way at other times in the day?*

Modifications

You can attempt the exercise standing closer to your horse when you become more comfortable dealing with:

- Intense emotions or thoughts that arise
- Calming your horse when they are distressed

Sharing the Present

Exercise #3: Body awareness near your horse

Body awareness near your horse

Shreyasi and Frank Brodhecker

Jennifer and Honey, photography by Erich Brodhecker

Sharing the Present

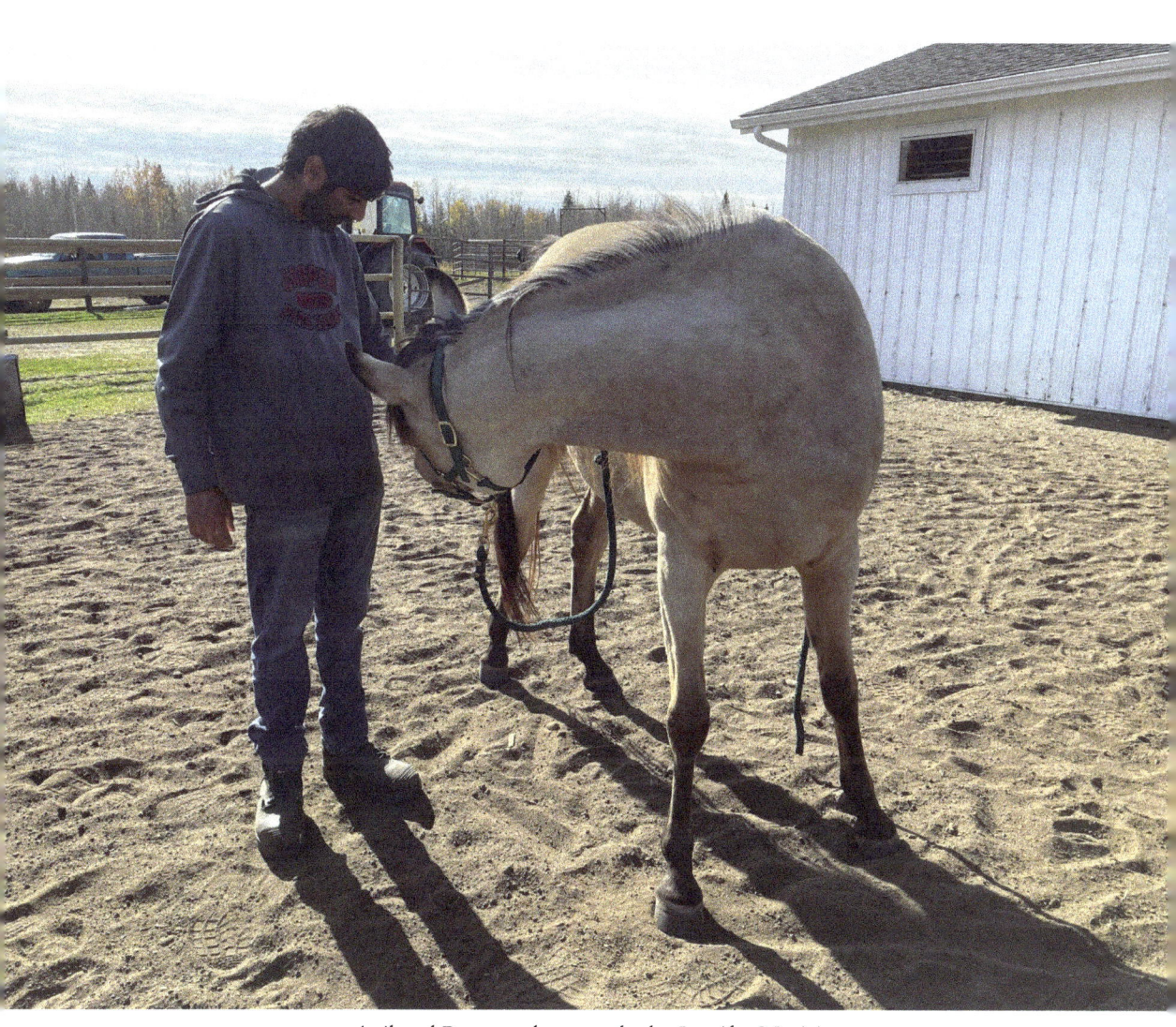

Anil and Romeo, photography by Jennifer Maciej

Intro

This is a body awareness exercise that expands beyond noticing breathing to noticing other physical sensations in your body, in a mindful way.

Context

First, across the fence; later, with your horse (briefly)

This is an exercise from MBSR, employed to develop paying mindful attention to your body. As you intentionally scan your body, bringing various areas into the field of attention, you may encounter pleasant, unpleasant, or neutral (neither pleasant nor unpleasant) sensations. Provided that you are not overwhelmed, we invite you to explore these, regardless of whether they are pleasant or unpleasant. This helps you begin relating to your body differently and to be fully present in your body (also called being "embodied"). Being embodied helps you to communicate genuinely with your horse, since that is how they experience present moments. If, at any time, you begin to feel overwhelmed, we encourage you to refer to the strategies in Chapter 3 of Section One.

As you start the exercise, begin by noticing the physical sensations inside your body from moment to moment, without trying to change them or push them away. You are later invited to notice the physical space between you and your horse, and the horse's body position and movements. Once you are used to this practice, you will find you can often do this in a few minutes, or longer, as you choose. You are welcome to take as long as needed, and you can introduce periods of quiet or silence into the guidance as well. Watching the video or listening to the audio file for this exercise may offer other perspectives.

We recommend practising the exercise at a distance from your horse, while they are in a pasture, paddock, or arena. You could also have your horse inside a stall while you stand outside the stall. This separation allows you to pay full attention to your internal experience without feeling distracted by your horse's movements. It also enables your physical safety, since feelings or emotions may arise that you will need to deal with on your own, before engaging with the horse. With this separation, your horse will not be as affected by your initial practice of the exercise.

If you would like to practise the exercise closer to your horse after some time, please refer to the modifications section. In this modified version, please keep your eyes open, stay standing, and always face the horse in the interests of safety. It's better not to have safety concerns when paying more attention to yourself than your horse, so have someone supervising you if needed.

When practising this exercise on your own (see modifications), sitting, standing, or lying down would also work. The eyes can be closed or slightly open with gaze lowered.

Possible reactions: Some people feel frustrated when they realize parts of their body feel uncomfortable or are in pain; your mind may focus on how your body used to be in the past or on what could be improved in some way. If this happens to you during this exercise, notice this frustration and acknowledge this as being your experience today. Appreciate that you are still willing to be present and tune in despite the discomfort you may experience at times during this exercise. If it is available, pay attention to your body *with gratitude*. Your body does a lot for you every day! Be patient, if you can, even if you are not entirely happy with your body in every moment.

Guidance

Phase 1/Body Scan: Attend to the sensations of breathing by tracking breathing in your whole body or in areas where the breath sensations are easy to follow. Continue breathing naturally, now focusing attention on your feet resting on the ground. Intentionally plant yourself on the earth, inviting the pelvis to sink and tilt slightly forward, straightening the spine, allowing the shoulders to gently ease back. Close your eyes or have them half closed and focused on the ground in front of you. Hold attention at your feet, noticing whether your feet are evenly bearing your weight, adjusting as needed and sensing the heels, soles, and toes inside your shoes. Curiously exploring the qualities of sensation in your feet, including tension, lightness, itchiness, or maybe something else. Pleasant or unpleasant qualities may exist at the same time; stay aware of these qualities as part of your experience of the present moment.

With the next exhale, release attention away from your feet. As you inhale, allow attention to travel up to your ankles and calves. Exploring whether there are physical sensations here, on both sides at once or on one side of the body and then the other. Observing at the surface of the skin and inside the body, at the front and back surfaces, and around the ankles and calves. If observing on one side and then the other, patiently note whether sensations are the same on each side or different. Registering qualities such as pressure, temperature changes, feelings of tension or ease. Shifting position if this feels right, noticing what your body is telling you.

Breathe out, letting go of attention at the level of the ankles and calves. Breathe in, placing attention on your knees, together or separately. As best you can, explore sensations in this region of the body. Thoughts or feelings can arise during this exercise, and when this happens, allow them to remain in the background while holding body sensations in the forefront of your attention.

Continue shifting attention upward along your legs, including the thighs and pelvis. At each area, briefly hold attention there and notice whether the area feels tight or relaxed or if there are other sensations. Approach your body with curiosity and openness, exploring what there is by sensing, not thinking. This is an exercise of exploration and discovery, and it is natural to take care of yourself as needed. If there are thoughts or reactions of feeling bored or frustrated, notice their presence before conveying attention back to the area of focus, currently being the thighs and pelvis.

Allow attention to now be placed upon the abdomen and chest. Although the core muscles in your abdomen are typically engaged when you ride, they may not draw attention when you are standing, sitting, or in another position. In this moment, observing small or large movements, areas of tension and ease. Observing your rate of breathing. Allow attention to now sweep around to your back and notice physical sensations in the lower and middle back, upper back, and shoulders. If there are tense areas that feel overwhelming, take care of yourself by stretching, massaging the sore area, or attending to breathing or another body part.

With the next exhale, let go of attending to the back. With the next inhale, place attention on your upper arms. Attending carefully to both arms together or separately. Detecting sensations in the upper arms, then through the elbows and forearms, and into your wrists and hands. Feeling, not thinking, about body sensations. Noticing the position of the arms and elbows, sensory qualities such as temperature and pressure on the surface and inside the arms. Noticing if the palms are facing up or down, whether the hands are clasped together or held in some other way.

Moving higher up through the body, gently drop attention into the neck and shoulders, resting in this area for some time and noting if there are sensations here. On the next inhale, shift attention into the face. Noticing temperature changes or other sensations across your face. Expanding awareness to also take in physical sensations on the top, back, and sides of your head.

Mindfully pay attention to your entire body, along the front of the body from the head to the feet, and then circling along the back of the body from the feet to the head. Notice physical sensations as they arise, stay a while, and then disappear. Taking in what is noticed both at the surface and inside the body. Note how it feels to be fully present in your body—embodied. If it is available, offer your body appreciation for what it *can* do, rather than what it *can't* do.

Phase 2: After completing this body scan, open your eyes if they were closed and continue to notice your body. Tune in to where your horse is. Noticing the physical space between you. Observing the quality of that space and how it feels. Now letting go of this practice, shift focus to something else as you complete this exercise.

Reflecting after the Exercise

- *What did you notice in this exercise?* This may include reactions of comfort or discomfort, evaluation of the exercise, physical sensations or emotions arising for you, your impressions of your horse, or something else.

- *How is this way of noticing your body different from usual?*

- *What do you think this exercise was like for your horse?* We encourage you to reflect on details observed in your horse's body language. Notice if this changes each time you practise the exercise.

- *Was it easier to notice your body, your horse's body, or both together?* Notice if this changes each time you practise the exercise.

- *How does this exercise affect how you feel about your horse, if at all? How might this way of being with your horse be helpful?*

Modifications

Here are several ideas for you to try:

With your horse

1. *Take a minute to notice one specific part of your body only.*

2. *Taking a few deep breaths, then tune in to the physical space between you and your horse in this moment.* Notice the feel and quality of this physical space between you and your horse. *Observe* your impressions, rather than *thinking* about them.

3. *Practise a parallel body awareness exercise.* Notice a part of your body, then notice the corresponding body part on your horse. For example, notice your left ear, then notice your horse's left ear and so on. Proceed through several parts, as you wish. As you intentionally relax one part of your body, observe whether there is relaxation in the corresponding body part of your horse.

On your own

4. *Practise a body scan on your own.* You can do this in a few minutes or spend more time on each body part, thus taking more time for the full scan. You can also focus on noticing physical sensations in certain parts of your body only, such as the feeling of air in your nostrils as you breathe in and out or your boots resting on the ground.

Exercise #4: Touch and connection

Touch between horse and human

Shreyasi and Frank Brodhecker

Touch and connection, Next to Wild Photography

Sharing the Present

Braxton and Violet, SJ Originals Photography

Stephanie, Shay Rayann Photography

Intro

In this exercise, you pay attention to touch—a primary form of communication. Practising Exercise 3 (Breathing and being with your horse) before Exercise #4 cultivates body awareness, which is an important prerequisite here.

Context

With your horse

Just as you watch your horse most of the time, you naturally touch them often as well. Horses are sensitive and have high degrees of sensory awareness. We usually touch horses who feel safe with us entering their space, unless we need to intervene for safety reasons. Touch can be direct, by using your hands or body when you are on the ground or riding your horse. Touch can also be indirect, using reins and bit, physical aids such as a crop or lunge whip, and via the energy and presence of your body. Direct and indirect touch are both powerful ways to feel connected to your horse.

> *Reflect on ways that you touch or physically connect with your horse throughout a session. How does your horse reciprocate?*

For equestrians, "feel" is another skill related to touch. This is a hard concept to define, tackled in various books on the subject. For us, "feel" has several meanings, all of which link to noticing your bodily sensations and the feel of your horse's body in the present moment. In the context of mindfulness, being able to sense your own bodily sensations and your horse's responses from moment to moment will help you to develop your "feeling capacity." This exercise introduces "feel" and links it to your body awareness from one moment to the next.

The term "neutral pelvis" appears in the exercise guidance, which comes from Centered Riding® and Connected Riding® approaches. This term refers to holding the pelvis in a position where the back is neither overly arched nor slumped forwards. To understand the neutral pelvis, sit on the edge of a chair and imagine you are growing a heavy tail from the base of your spine. Alternatively, while standing, imagine growing heavy tree roots from your pelvis into the ground, weighting or pulling you down so that your body rests closer to the earth. These visuals tend to shift your pelvis into a neutral position. If you need further assistance to better understand what this means, please refer to the equestrian resources at the end of Chapter 1 of Section One. We also include a diagram in the next exercise, Exercise #5: Grooming your horse mindfully.

> *Feel is about sensing, not thinking.*

This is the first exercise in which we encourage you to be near your horse from the start. If you prefer, you can watch our video of this exercise before attempting it yourself. You can also use the audio file when you are with your horse or have someone read this guidance out loud to you.

Please remember that your safety and your horse's safety are paramount. Do only what feels comfortable for you, and what seems to keep the horse calm and relaxed. This exercise can be tried in various ways:

- Your horse may be at liberty and move freely if you know them well.
- Someone can hold the horse for you, so that the horse is still able to move around.
- Your horse can be haltered and loosely tied, while you monitor for signs of stress and adjust accordingly.

Remember and practice the safety guidelines discussed—whether you are alone with your horse, with supervision, or near other horses (for example, if you practise this exercise with your horse in the field).

Your energy and body language help the horse you are spending time with decide whether you are safe to be around. Because horses are prey animals, they experience your touch as intimate, regardless of how long you've known them. Thus, it is important to adopt a calm, non-threatening energy and wait until your horse appears relaxed before touching them. Please review the calming exercise in the Foundation Exercise (Chapter 5 of Section Two) if needed. Once you feel relaxed and have also observed relaxation in your horse's body language (soft eyes, licking or chewing, head down, or other signs described in Chapter 3 of Section One), approach and touch your horse.

If you observe, through touch and body language signals that your horse appears stressed or tense, decide how best to proceed. Attempt to calm your horse through soft words and/or gentle touch at areas that the horse is comfortable with. Avoid sensitive areas. Pay attention to whether your horse is backing away from touch due to sensitivity or anxiety; if so, try the strategies in Chapter 3 of Section One to calm a stressed horse. Remember to watch for safety issues and ensure that the horse continues to respect your personal space.

> *Staying engaged with your horse:*
>
> - Be aware of the movements and shifts in body space as you and your horse approach or back away from each other.
>
> - Calm your horse by talking in a calm, soft voice, blinking slowly and using soft eyes, relaxing your body purposefully, yawning and stroking the withers, and/or getting the horse moving.

Possible reactions: People often let their guard down more easily around animals, which can make your experience during this exercise more immediate and intense. Your encounters with the horse may stir memories or reflections on how physical closeness plays a role in your human relationships or your relationships with other horses or animals. These are all experiences that you can remain curious to in the moment.

Remember that if you feel overwhelmed, please take a few deep breaths, and wait until you feel more relaxed before refocusing on the activity or ending the activity. You could decide to revisit it later. Please connect with trusted friends or mental health professionals if observations arise for which you need support. Simple interactions with horses can be immensely powerful—and these awareness exercises may elicit unexpected outcomes.

Guidance

Phase 1: Standing across the fence, take a few moments to notice your breathing sensations. Noticing with curiosity and openness and with the next exhale, release attention from your breathing. Feel your feet anchoring you to the ground and the sensations of being supported by the earth. Turning a soft-eyed gaze towards your horse, set the intention to approach them.

Sharing the Present

As you begin moving, notice physical sensations of movement and pay attention to body language in your horse. For example, noticing the position of their ears, their facial expression, body posture, tail, and legs. Taking in signs of relaxation or discomfort or other signs that may be present. If your horse looks up at you or moves away, stop for a moment to breathe deeply in and out, and then practise soft eyes while slowly approaching again. Repeat this movement every time they move away. If your horse is standing still and welcoming you into their space, proceed with slow intention to finally stand beside them.

Phase 2: Once you are positioned beside your horse, place attention at the area of your heart, noticing emotions in this moment. Allow your pelvis to drop into neutral position, so your back is not arched overly forward or backward. With soft eyes, touch your horse at a place comfortable for them, such as at the neck or shoulders. Pausing here, resting one or both hands, marking the feel of your horse's body under your hand(s), with palm, fingers, or sides of the hands on their coat. Continually noticing the physical response in your body and how your horse is responding to this touch. If thoughts or emotions become noticeable, identify them before gently shifting attention back to the sense of touch.

If this seems comfortable for you and your horse, allow your hand(s) to now rest at one place, then intentionally move them across the surface of your horse's body to rest again at another place. Exploring if your horse's muscles are soft or tight, whether they seem accepting of touch, or whether they lean into touch at certain areas. If you and your horse appear comfortable, experiment with varying the type of touch, for example scratching them in specific areas. If they lean into you, reclaim your space gently and firmly, by shifting their position or signalling a boundary with your posture (for example, placing your arms in front of you).

Taking care of your horse is part of this practice. If they seem uneasy or stressed, then practise soft eyes, deep breathing, or touch another area before gradually revisiting the original body part. Curiously exploring while respecting their comfort.

Stepping away now, keep your eyes on your horse as you leave their location. Once you are across the fence, if it is available, extend gratitude to your horse for participating in this exercise. Notice how your body feels at this point in time, noticing physical sensations, tuning into thoughts or emotions, and then breathing deeply in and out. Resume your natural pace of breathing; then, on the next exhale, let go of this exercise.

Reflecting after the Exercise

- *What did you notice in this exercise?* This may include reactions of comfort or discomfort, evaluations of the exercise, physical sensations or emotions arising for you, your impressions of your horse, or something else.

- *How is this way of touching your horse different than usual?*

- *What do you think this exercise was like for your horse?* We encourage you to reflect on details observed in your horse's body language. Notice if this changes each time you practise the exercise.

- *How does this exercise affect how you feel about your horse, if at all? How might this way of being with your horse be helpful?*

> *Reflect on the feelings of vulnerability that may arise for you as you touch your horse.*

Modifications

Here are a few ideas for you to try:

1. *Vary the time.* Practise this for as long as you like or for only a few minutes. Brief sessions are a good chance to deliberately notice the feel of your horse's mane, for example. In these short periods if your horse is relaxed try focusing on other specific body parts.

2. *Vary the part of your body you focus on.* Experiment with noticing physical sensations in your arms and various other parts of your body as you hug your horse, or when using indirect touch like reins, halter, and/or lead rope. Later exercises will focus on the physical sensations of standing, leading, or riding your horse.

Sharing the Present

Exercise #5: Grooming your horse mindfully

Grooming

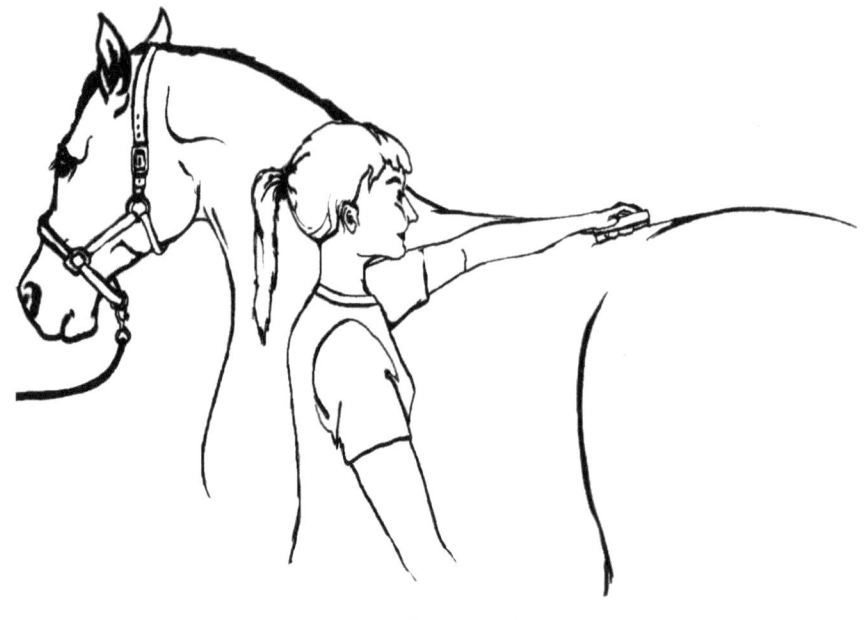

Grooming (2)

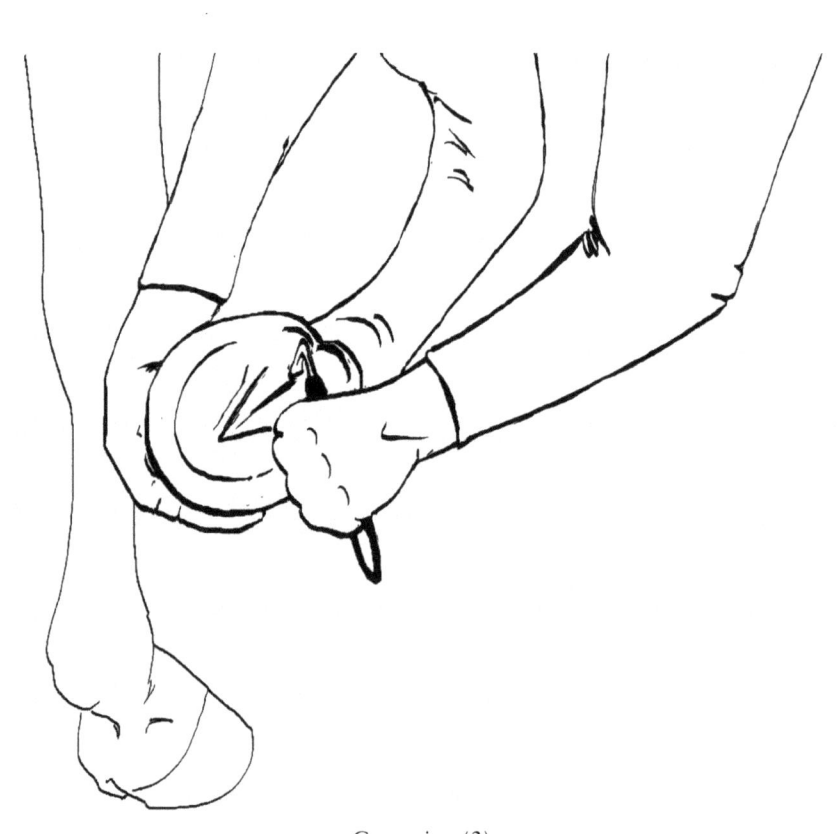

Grooming (3)

Sharing the Present

Neutral pelvis

Sush and Stella, Next to Wild Photography

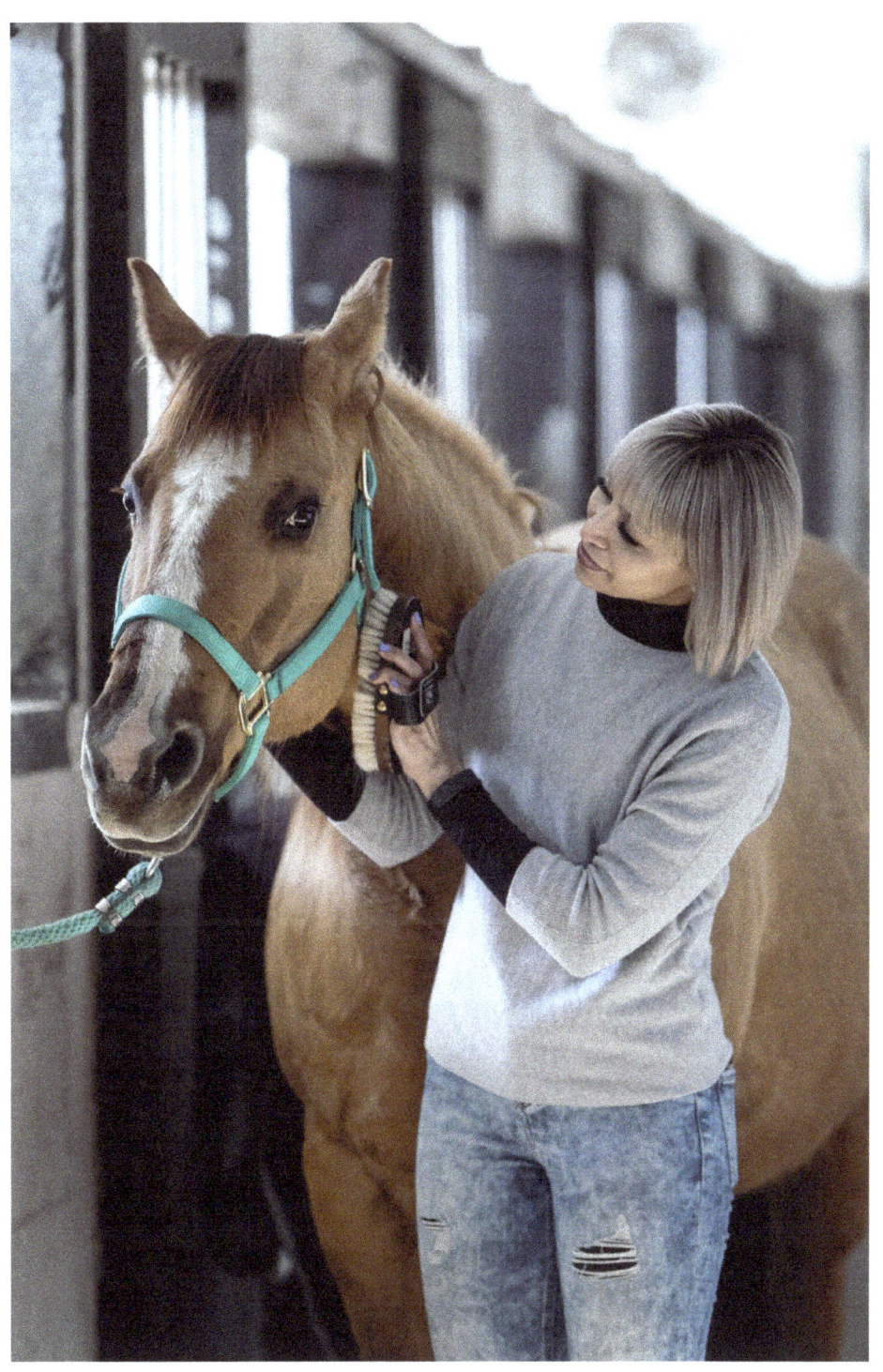

Sharing the Present

Sush and Stella (2), Next to Wild Photography

Intro

This exercise is a particular extension of Exercise 4, where touch, in the context of grooming, is an opportunity to practise mindfulness with your horse. An alternative is to mindfully watch another person grooming at certain points in the exercise. This exercise employs the five senses and a particular way of conceptualizing mindful awareness: OBSERVE-DESCRIBE-PARTICIPATE.

You can read the guidance ahead of time or have someone read it to you during the exercise. You could also watch the video or listen to the audio file of the exercise for enhanced understanding.

Context

With your horse

During this activity, you have a chance to practise the "WHAT" skills of mindfulness. Dr. Marsha Linehan describes these skills as "*observe, describe, participate*" in her mindfulness module for Dialectical Behavior Therapy (Linehan, 2015). Specifically, you can do the following:

- OBSERVE with your five senses during the exercise—this is included in the guidance.

- DESCRIBE the facts of your observations—if you choose to describe during the exercise, briefly and intentionally noting your observations while staying connected to your horse, not getting stuck in thoughts. If you notice this is too distracting, then letting go of this process. Describing can also happen through journaling observations immediately after the exercise.

- PARTICIPATE by immersing yourself fully in this moment and this activity—this is included in the guidance.

> *Don't just go through the motions: Bring attention to what is happening in the present moment.*

Remember to practise safe handling and to monitor your horse's body language throughout the exercise. You can bring your horse to your grooming spot *before* starting this exercise.

Guidance

Attend to breath sensations, feeling the air enter and leave your entire body, or placing focus at an area of the body where breath sensations are easy to notice. Anchor your feet on the ground, feeling the sensations of your feet on the earth. Once positioned beside your horse, place attention at your heart, noticing emotions in this moment. Allow your pelvis to drop into neutral position, so your back is not overly arched, forward, or backward. With soft eyes and a clear gaze, now touch your horse at a place comfortable for them, such as at the neck or shoulders. Pausing here, resting one or both hands, marking the feel of your horse's body under your hand(s).

Bring attention now to the five senses as you set the intention of grooming your horse. Begin by *watching* their body. If they seem stressed, take some deep breaths while relaxing your body and speaking in a calm voice. With soft eyes, notice the grooming kit—the shapes, colours, and textures of the grooming tools. As you groom, watch for patterns on your horse's coat created by the tools and dust or hair rising through the process. Watch for signs of relaxation or discomfort in your horse, adjusting by grooming another area and re-approaching certain body parts as needed for their comfort. Also paying attention to your comfort.

Next notice *sounds* in the surroundings as you are grooming. Hearing grooming tools on your horse's body, your own breathing, and the sounds of your horse, such as sighing or exhales.

Tuning in now to the sensations of *smell* or *taste* around you. With the next exhale, release attention from the senses of smell and taste and attend to sensations of *touch* as you groom your horse. Notice physical sensations in your hands as you rest them on your horse's shoulder, withers, or neck. Registering other body sensations arising or changes in your horse's body language through this process. Continue adjusting your grooming and body position for both your comfort.

As you groom, invite thoughts or emotions to now enter your field of attention. Perhaps noticing joy, impatience, or something else. Leaving these thoughts and emotions in the background, escort your attention back to the primary focus of grooming your horse. With the next exhale, take a step away while releasing attention from grooming.

Reflecting after the Exercise

- *What did you notice in this exercise?* This may include reactions of comfort or discomfort, evaluation of the exercise, physical sensations or emotions arising for you, your impressions of your horse, or something else.

- *How is this way of grooming your horse different than usual?*

- *What do you think this exercise was like for your horse?* We encourage you to reflect on details observed in your horse's body language. Notice if this changes each time you practise the exercise.

- *How does this exercise affect how you feel about your horse, if at all? How might this way of being with your horse be helpful?*

Modifications

Groom your horse in different environments and notice the differing sensory exposures.

1. *Try various tying contexts*—such as grooming your horse while your horse is ground tied instead of tied to a rail. Compare the experiences.

2. *Groom your horse while loose, depending on your comfort and experience level*; for example, while they are still in the pasture and untied, if you are comfortable with your horse. This may be a different experience than grooming while they are haltered.

3. *Incorporate awareness of the textures and scents of some of the grooming products you use on your horse*—such as detangler or fly spray. In this way, noticing your five senses while you groom your horse.

Sharing the Present

Exercise #6: Moving with your horse

Motion with your horse

Shreyasi and Frank Brodhecker

Exploring the world together, Next to Wild Photography

Intro

This exercise is mindfully noticing how you move with your horse.

Context

With your horse

Building on the earlier exercises, you are invited to stay mindfully aware during movement with your horse. Movement can be in the context of structured activities, such as when you are leading or lunging your horse, or simply moving with your horse from one place to another. You might notice movement in several ways. For example, you could notice your body moving, how your movements influence your horse's movements and vice versa, the physical space between you both as you move, or something else.

This exercise and Exercise #7, Riding mindfully, are to help equestrians of all levels to bring moments of mindfulness to their structured time with horses. We appreciate that reading the guidance may not be possible during these activities for safety reasons. We therefore have video and audio files for you to explore and encourage you to practice mindful noticing for a few moments to start. Remember that this is about connecting with your horse in a different way and there is no timeline to do that.

From a safety perspective, practise how to safely lead your horse with supervision *before* trying this exercise and ask for help during the exercise, as necessary. To start, we recommend that your horse be haltered during this exercise. You can make haltering your horse part of mindful noticing if you like.

You may want to walk with your horse outside of the paddock or pasture, inside an arena, or within the field. Whichever location you choose, keep in mind that if other horses are nearby you must remain aware of their presence and follow safety rules. You may also have the opportunity to mindfully notice the dynamic between your horse and the rest of the herd if they are nearby.

Possible reactions: Your feelings might change each time you try this exercise—sometimes you may enjoy it and at other times you may not. Whatever your experience is in the present moment, it is entirely okay. There is no right or wrong way to feel. If you do notice intense reactions, allow yourself to realize what you're thinking and feeling before returning focus back to the exercise.

> *Sensing, not thinking*
>
> *Don't judge your judging; be kind to yourself as you practise noticing in a mindful way.*

Guidance

Phase 1/Approach: Taking a few deep breaths in and out, allow your breathing to settle into a natural pace and rhythm. Tracking breathing sensations in the entire body or at a place where breathing feels easily noticed, for example in the nostrils, chest, or stomach. Now feel your feet anchoring you to the ground. Start approaching your horse, pausing if they move away or seem uneasy. During a pause, watch with soft eyes, breathe deeply, and speak gently to your horse, if you choose, before resuming your approach. Take your time, waiting for your horse to invite you into their space. When positioned beside your horse, halter them with your full attention.

Phase 2/Movement: After haltering your horse, take a moment to notice your feet and their hooves planted on the earth. Sinking into a neutral pelvis, notice if your lead-holding hand is turned to face the sky or the ground. Setting the intention to move with your horse, notice exactly when you begin moving. Pay close attention to your body moving through space, widening the field of attention to include careful noticing of your horse's movements. Notice your body as you walk straight or in curves.

Phase 3/The Space between you: As the horse moves with you, observe whether your movements together are fluid. Feel whether your horse senses your cues and follows through. Noticing the give and take of pressure and release if that is how you communicate. If you notice a lack of connection with your horse, try slowing down, practising simpler movements, or pausing to regroup. If your horse appears stressed, speaking in a soft voice, blinking slowly, yawning, or relaxing your body by releasing muscle tension are all options. Continue feeling your body move with your horse. You may experiment with changing pace and direction, occasionally stopping and starting movement, noting how you communicate and how your horse responds. After the next exhale, let go of your attention to this exercise.

Reflecting after the Exercise

- *What did you notice in this exercise?* This may include reactions of comfort or discomfort, evaluations of the exercise, physical sensations or emotions arising for you, your impressions of your horse, or something else.

- *How is this way of moving with your horse different than usual?*

- *How did the physical space (and/or energy) shift between you and your horse during the exercise? How willing was your horse to take your lead and how did this show up?*

- *What do you think this exercise was like for your horse?* We encourage you to reflect on details observed in your horse's body language. Notice if this changes each time you practise the exercise.

- *How does this exercise affect how you feel about your horse, if at all? How might this way of being with your horse be helpful?*

Modifications

Here are some ideas for variation:

1. *Take moments to be aware in the present moment when you walk your horse from point A to point B.*

2. *Walk with your horse at liberty in the pasture.* If you plan to try this exercise, it is safest to be in the pasture when no other horses are present or in an arena or round pen without another horse.

3. *Walk your horse with a rope first, then untie the rope and continue to walk with your horse while they are free to move at liberty.* If you are unfamiliar with liberty concepts, you can try the exercise with

your horse when they are free and un-haltered. This will entail some change, as it is likely you will be mirroring your horse and moving as they walk. Or you may shift to simply *being with* your horse if they stop walking.

4. *Introduce moments of mindful awareness at times you are not practising* this exercise (while walking or when practising specific movements on the ground). For example, periodically tuning in to your body or the energy projected from you to the horse, tuning in to their responses and energy, intentionally adjusting your movements in some way and registering the impact on the horse.

Leading your horse

Sharing the Present

Frank and Rhianna, Next to Wild Photography

Shreyasi and Frank Brodhecker

Shreyasi and Grace, Next to Wild Photography

Sharing the Present

Walking with your horse

Erich and Anise, photography by Jennifer Maciej

Sharing the Present

Katie Hembree, Heart of a Cowgirl Photography

Shreyasi and Frank Brodhecker

Erich and Joe, Amanda Ubell Photography

Sharing the Present

Erich and Violet, photography by Jennifer Maciej

> *Body awareness helps you to notice "feel," which improves your timing when you apply pressure and release.*

> *What does leadership with your horse mean to you? Do you tend to be aggressive, passive, or both? Can you be assertive?*

Exercise #7: Riding mindfully—Being one with your horse while riding

Riding mindfully, Stephanie Dewes, Shay Rayann Photography

Riding mindfully (2), photography by Jennifer Maciej

Sharing the Present

Riding mindfully (3), photography by Rhonda Bignell

Riding mindfully (4), Katie Hembree, Heart of a Cowgirl Photography

Riding mindfully (5), Katie Hembree, Heart of a Cowgirl Photography

Sharing the Present

Riding mindfully (6), Katie Hembree, Heart of a Cowgirl Photography

Riding mindfully (7), photography by Rhonda Bignell

Intro

This exercise is intended for those with riding experience, although it accommodates both novice and seasoned riders, various riding disciplines, and different gaits or riding movements. When you first try this, you may only be able to attend mindfully for a few moments during your riding time (owing to distractions, feeling overwhelmed, etc.). Even a few moments of noticing this way is still part of the practice. As you continue practising, you can attend mindfully for longer time periods. We invite you to read the guidance and listen to the guided audio file for this exercise before attempting this exercise for a few moments during your next ride.

Context

With your horse

This is a mindful movement exercise in which you can intentionally bring noticing, in a particular way, to moments of riding. Equestrians already employ these practices, although they do not necessarily use the same language. As you may know, there are some suggestions included in the guidance that are influenced by Centered Riding® and Connected Riding® (resources offered in Chapter 1 of Section One).

The intent of this exercise is to notice body sensations in yourself and your horse for even a brief portion of your riding. Noticing body sensations can help with "feel." Although we don't explicitly define this concept, present-moment focus is essential to detecting it, whether you are on the ground or riding. Identifying your physical sensations, maintaining embodied awareness—that is, being fully present in your body—and offering more subtle cues in your seat, hands, and legs while riding is practising mindfulness of body. Such skills fine-tune the conversation you have with your horse.

This exercise starts with your horse standing still and then advances to riding movements. We suggest riding at a pace you are comfortable with, as the purpose of the exercise is to *notice in a certain way*. Mindful awareness can be practised at any gait, including when your horse is standing or walking. Tuning in to your physical sensations and subsequently adjusting your body can affect the quality of your riding. Even a few moments of being mindfully aware of your body and your horse can make a big difference, particularly in a high-stress situation.

Possible reactions: Occasionally, bringing body awareness to riding can trigger trauma responses or memories. Although this is unlikely to happen, if you do notice such memories, please take care of yourself using the strategies mentioned in Chapter 3 of Section One. Dismount safely from your horse, if possible. Journaling, speaking to trusted others about your experience, and seeking professional mental health assistance are also recommended.

Guidance

Phase 1/Stillness: With your horse stationary, notice your breathing and watch with soft eyes. Tune in to the physical sensations of being seated in the saddle, noticing if your pelvis is in a neutral position, and adjusting as needed. Sinking so that the pubic bone descends while your spine straightens, feeling stable and secure in your seat. Notice the shoulders relaxing. Now sense physical sensations in the thighs and calves, intentionally relaxing your legs. Rest the ball of each foot deeper in its stirrup, adjusting the position of your feet as needed. Register physical sensations of the reins against your fingers, shifting position to detect soft contact with your horse's mouth (if they are receptive to such contact). After assuming this balanced and relaxed seat, set the intention to look ahead, and communicate to your horse to start moving.

Phase 2/Movement: As your horse moves, abide in balanced stillness in your seat as you navigate through movement (your horse moving now at a walk). Registering physical sensations in your pelvis and in the rest of the body, including the core, legs, and arms. Compassionately adjusting your body so that you feel in sync with your horse, staying relaxed, yet purposeful. If physical discomfort arises, decide whether you want to ride through it or adjust your body position while your horse is moving or still.

If transitioning up and down through different gaits, notice how your body feels through these transitions. Paying specific attention to how your pelvis, back, neck, and shoulders shift in position and tension over time. Tune in to body sensations and the physical sensations of breathing as you continue riding, even if you can do so for just a few moments.

Phase 3/Physical connection between you and your horse: Widen the field of attention to now include your body sensations and your horse's responses. Noticing how you implement and vary cues as needed. If your attention turns to emotions or thoughts, notice this before returning your primary focus to your body movements and those of your horse from one moment to the next. Pausing or stopping movement as needed, experimenting with direction and pace, as comfortable. If you are overwhelmed, take a few moments to notice your breathing before resuming the focus on body sensations in you both. At any point in the ride, with the next exhale, let go of this exercise to focus on the next moment.

Modifications

Here are a few ideas to vary this activity:

1. *Have someone you trust lead your horse at a walk.* This gives you an opportunity to briefly close your eyes during the exercise.

2. *Ride bareback, if you are comfortable doing so,* and notice any differences in your riding experience.

3. Introduce *moments of mindful awareness at times you are not practising* this exercise, when possible and within your level of riding comfort, such as in an indoor riding arena, an outdoor arena, or on the trail.

Exercise #8: Noticing thoughts and emotions—Expectations, judgments, and feelings

Thoughts and emotions

Sharing the Present

Thoughts and emotions (2)

Joe's sentience, SJ Originals Photography

Intro

This exercise develops your ability to notice thoughts and emotions that may be present and then release them as you choose.

Context

Initially, on your own; later, across the fence; finally, during brief moments with your horse

In the exercises so far, you have focused on the five senses of sight, taste, touch, sound, and smell while in the company of your horse. You have also focused on your breathing and bodily sensations, and on movement with your horse. In those exercises, if thoughts or emotions arose in your awareness, you noticed them before shifting attention back to the focus of the exercise.

In this exercise, you will *purposely* pay attention to your thoughts and emotions. In other words, this is the time for them to be released from the imaginary container. You may find that—just as with body sensations—thoughts and emotions appear, persist, and eventually pass. Practising this way of observing your thoughts and emotions strengthens your ability to cope when challenging thoughts or intense emotions arise. With practice, you can observe and be with thoughts and emotions without getting caught up in their intensity.

As we practise, we start to accurately notice the facts of a situation and the typical ways we react under stress. Mindfulness helps us to build skills to intentionally choose how to act in a situation, i.e., we learn to *respond*. This has huge benefits for coping with stressful events, which is a key principle of MBSR.

> *Thoughts and emotions are just information—so you can choose how to deal with them.*

This can apply to situations at the barn and in other parts of your life. For example, noticing when you judge yourself or your horse, feel distressing emotions, such as shame and guilt, and have urges to "fix" other people's (or a horse's) behaviours or feelings. This exercise also helps you to pinpoint when you may be inaccurately reading your horse's emotions or feel overly responsible for your horse's feelings.

As we mentioned in Chapter 3 of Section One, people find it hard to know the difference between thoughts and emotions. This exercise is an opportunity to understand those differences. This is practised on your own with *indirect benefits* on the connection with your horse.

What are these benefits? When you become aware of judgments and strong emotions, you can act from a place of clarity. Clarity allows your horse to feel safe. This practice also helps you to notice your horse's emotions, which may have nothing to do with you, and choose how to respond in those moments. Accurately noticing their emotions more of the time helps to improve the connection.

The guidance in this exercise uses visual metaphors—such as the riverbank or conveyor belt analogies mentioned in Chapter 2 of Section One —to help you understand how mindfully paying attention to your thoughts and emotions works. They demonstrate that you can be close enough to see the thoughts and emotions, but not so close that you are mired in them. We hope that this makes sense after practising. As with the other mindful practices, we provide an audio file of this exercise at www.mindfulmarewellness.com to deepen your experience.

Possible reactions: You may be surprised at the thoughts and emotions that arise during this exercise. It is common to feel frustrated or disappointed at times. Noticing in the present moment means you are being mindful regardless and there is no right or wrong way to feel in a mindful practice. We invite you to be gentle with yourself on this journey of self-awareness.

Guidance

Phase 1: Notice sensations of the breath in your entire body or at an area where the breath is most noticeable, such as in the nostrils, chest, or abdomen. Now focus on feeling the ground beneath your feet. Rest in this awareness for as long as you choose. Releasing attention from your feet, start noticing thoughts or emotions present now. Like other sensations, thoughts and emotions arise, persist, and fade away. With curiosity and patience, notice thoughts and emotions as if they are clouds crossing the sky. You can label them as pleasant, unpleasant, or neutral, and explore their content. If you feel overwhelmed, step away from thoughts and emotions to focus on your breathing.

Phase 2: If you choose, invite an image of your horse into your exercise and observe thoughts and emotions arising in response to this image. Bringing openness and curiosity to what arises for you. With the next exhale, let go of this picture of your horse to again notice breathing sensations. When you are ready, let go of this practice to focus on something else.

Reflecting after the Exercise

- *What did you notice in this exercise?* This may include reactions of comfort or discomfort, evaluations of the exercise, physical sensations or emotions arising for you, your impressions of your horse, or something else.

- *Did you notice any thoughts or emotions arising about your horse that surprised you?*

- *How does this exercise affect how you feel about your horse, if at all? How might practising this exercise affect the time you spend with your horse in the future?*

Modifications

Here are some variations for you to try:

On your own

1. *Tune in to your thoughts and emotions at other times of the day.*

2. *Use journaling as another way to record your present-moment observations.*

Near your horse (provided they can move away if they prefer)

3. *Briefly allow your primary focus of attention to rest on thoughts or emotions in the present moment.* Notice the qualities of these thoughts or emotions (such as the content or whether the experience is pleasant, unpleasant or neither), notice breathing sensations if you are overwhelmed, and then let go of this practice. The intent of this is to bring awareness to factors affecting the interaction with your horse right now.

4. *Try noticing your horse's body language over time, including the interaction between the two of you.* Notice the thoughts or emotions this brings up for you, briefly, before returning to visually noticing your horse's behaviours.

> *Reflect on how your horse has shown you emotions. Which emotions have you noticed?*

Sharing the Present

Exercise #9: Being thankful for your horse

Honey, SJ Originals Photography

Thankful, Katie Hembree, Heart of a Cowgirl Photography

Sharing the Present

Anise, SJ Originals Photography

Intro

This exercise focuses on "lovingkindness" and gratitude exercises, which resemble those used in some mindfulness-based therapies and meditative traditions. The intent of this exercise is to cultivate feelings of gratitude and caring for your horse, if this feels comfortable.

Context

On your own, if you can hold an image of your horse in mind throughout; *with your horse,* after considerable independent practice.

"Lovingkindness" originates from the Pali word *metta* and generally refers to feelings of positive regard for the people in your life. In this exercise, you will direct these loving emotions towards your horse. Exercises such as this can have a significant impact on the quality of connection with your horse.

If you prefer to use other language, words you can use are "caring" or "kindness." Please mentally substitute these or similar words as we explain this activity and provide guidance. We invite you to attempt this exercise with an open mind and observe if this has any impact on your connection to your horse. As with other exercises, we provide an audio file of the exercise at www.mindfulmarewellness.com to deepen your experience.

Possible reactions: This exercise can be overwhelming, depending on past relationship experiences and your degree of comfort with giving and receiving such feelings. This is an awareness exercise, and there is no perfect way to feel. Be gentle and patient with whatever arises, and if you need extra support, consider speaking to someone you trust, or seek professional help.

Guidance

Phase 1: Notice breathing sensations in the entire body or at a point in the body where the breath sensations feel most noticeable, such as in the nostrils, throat, chest, or abdomen. Imagine being near your horse and noticing their physical appearance. Allow your attention to again alight on breathing sensations, taking your time. If you are on your own, gently close your eyes or leave them half closed and focused on a spot on the ground in front of you. Now place your attention onto feelings for your horse. If it feels natural, begin radiating caring feelings toward your horse. Alternately, imagine providing affection in other ways, such as by stroking their neck or talking to them.

As you radiate this caring, try adding words to your emotions (if this fits for you). "May you be healthy," "May you be happy," "May you be safe." The words matter less than the feelings of compassion and gratitude that accompany them. Reflect on how much your life has changed for the better since you met your horse. If these feelings are not available, notice this and honour where you are. In this case, continue to notice breathing while you imagine being near your horse.

Phase 2: Notice the state of your body right now. Are there body sensations and do they stay the same or change over time? If you choose to, notice thoughts and emotions present. If you are overwhelmed, take care of yourself by breathing deeply, encouraging yourself, or focusing on one of the five senses to feel grounded.

Returning your attention to the image of your horse, again radiate caring feelings to them. If you'd like, imagine them radiating such feelings back to you. If this feels uncomfortable, allow yourself to focus on your breathing or anything else that you choose. On the next exhale, open your eyes (if they are closed) to let go of this exercise.

Reflecting after the Exercise

- *What did you notice in this exercise?* This may include reactions of comfort or discomfort, evaluations of the exercise, physical sensations or emotions arising for you, your impressions of your horse, or something else.

- *Did you notice any thoughts or emotions arising that surprised you?*

- *How does this exercise affect how you feel about your horse, if at all? How might practising this exercise affect the time you later spend with your horse?*

Modifications

Here are some ways you can vary this activity:

On your own

1. *Change the words or don't use words at all.* Instead, you can imagine your feelings as a field or beam of light, as feelings of warmth, or as a blanket.

2. *Imagine your horse extending unconditional love and anticipate how it feels to receive this love and acceptance.* If this is challenging for you, try imagining your horse showing their feelings for you by similarly sending you light, feelings of warmth, or a blanket.

3. *Notice whether practising this exercise on your own makes you feel differently than when you are with your horse.* Sometimes, such gratitude exercises build empathy. Are you better able to see things from your horse's point of view after doing this exercise? Perhaps it helps you understand more easily what your horse is communicating in various situations. If this isn't your experience, this is okay.

Near your horse

4. *Briefly focus on feelings of gratitude when you are with your horse,* if this feels spontaneous and genuine. This is another way to see the world through your horse's eyes, and it may even offer insight into how to approach a particular situation differently. At the least, over time, it helps to deepen your emotional attachment to them.

In your everyday life

5. After practising this exercise with your horse, you may be interested in trying other forms of lovingkindness meditation. Some versions invite you to practise feelings of positive regard for people in your life for whom you have no intense feelings (the neutral person) and those for whom you have conflicted feelings (the difficult person). We include links to such meditations in the mindfulness references listed at the end of Chapter 2 in Section One, including some audio resources.

Sharing the Present

Exercise #10: Letting go

Letting go

Fiona running, SJ Originals Photography

Sharing the Present

Lucky close up, Prairie Darkroom Photography

Intro

This exercise will help you cope with distressing thoughts or emotions arising when you face challenges or difficult moments with your horse, including those of frustration or grief. Attempt this exercise only in such situations. If this does not apply, please move on to another exercise. You can read the script or listen to the audio file at www.mindfulmarewellness.com as you choose.

Context

Definitely, *on your own*

This exercise is designed for you to mindfully notice difficult moments in the relationship with your horse. There can be a variety of situations in which this applies. There may be moments of frustration with how you or your horse are, your horse may be suffering an illness, or it may be time to say goodbye for various reasons. All these situations can be painful, but a mindfulness practice will help you cope with this type of event.

Mindfulness skills help to navigate the complex thoughts and emotions that arise at these times. Even though you must let go of certain aspects of the relationship—especially if your horse is no longer with you—you can continue to hold on to positive memories of how your horse improved your life. In this way, practise both holding on and letting go.

> *Letting go in a relationship involves acceptance and release.*

Possible reactions: Before beginning, consider whether this exercise will be helpful to you. We include it here because letting go is a part of life, and this exercise highlights how mindfulness benefits this part of your journey. For some, paying mindful attention to a few breaths is enough to experience the process of letting go. For others, this mindful awareness is only a small part of their letting-go process.

Guidance

Notice your breathing from one moment to the next. Resting attention on the physical sensations of breathing, in each present moment. Staying curious and accepting of whatever makes itself known to you. Gently close your eyes or leave them half closed and focused on a spot on the ground in front of you. If there are thoughts or emotions arising, let these remain in the background while breathing sensations are in the foreground. If you are overwhelmed, take care of yourself by adjusting body position or noticing breathing for as long as you'd like.

Now invite a picture of you and your horse into your mind's eye. Continue holding this image and start noticing thoughts or emotions arising in response. Let yourself notice whatever arises, as best you can. If memories of the good and bad times you've had with your horse surface, stay present to these. If it feels right to you, imagine watching your horse in this picture with gratitude and an open heart. Speaking any words you'd like to say to them. Imagine you and your horse together, and your energies as one. Envisioning them as safe and loved, wherever they may be.

If you feel overwhelmed, shift your attention to breathing sensations or one of the five senses. Attending to what you see, hear, smell, taste, and touch right now. If it is available, imagine yourself letting things be, and thereby letting go. Forcing this process is not necessary, rather honour your experience exactly as it is. With the next exhale, open your eyes (if they are closed) and let go of this exercise.

Modifications

If you are selling your horse, you could adjust this activity to include imagining them living in a safe and loving home with their new owner. You could envision yourself and the new owner interacting positively with each other, as you both share the bond of caring for this horse at different stages of their life.

Exercise #11: Putting it all together

Putting it all together

Sharing the Present

Joe running free, Amanda Ubell Photography

Intro

In this exercise you practise expanding your capacity to be mindfully aware of multiple aspects of your present experience. You can read the script or listen to the audio file of this exercise at www.mindfulmarewellness.com as you choose.

Context

On your own

The exercises to this point have invited you to focus attention on one thing at a time:

- Vision, touch, or one of your other senses
- Your bodily state
- Activities like walking or riding
- Your mental and emotional landscape

And returning to this chosen focus should you be distracted.

In this exercise, you will broaden that focus to notice *everything* arising in the present moment, not just one thing. There is no perfect way to do this exercise. If you set the intention to be aware and open-minded, and can focus on the present, even briefly, that's enough to complete this exercise.

> *Mindful awareness can mean focusing on just one thing—or staying aware of several things at once in the present moment.*

If this seems hard for you, please don't judge yourself. We include this exercise so that, if you would like, you can have a brief experience of this type of mindful awareness. As with the other exercises in this book, practise this only if you feel comfortable doing so. Your practice can just be noticing one thing at a time if this exercise doesn't work for you.

Guidance

Phase 1: Start by noticing the sensations of breathing in the entire body or in an area where it is easily noticed, such as in the nostrils, chest, or abdomen. Noticing the sensations of the air entering and leaving your body as you breathe in and out. Allow your eyes to be gently closed or half closed and focus on a spot on the ground in front of you. Now release attention from breathing and start noticing physical sensations in the entire body. If there are physical sensations, noting where they are in the body and their specific qualities, such as tension, ease, temperature changes, and so forth. As best you can, attending to such physical sensations, regardless of whether they are pleasant, unpleasant, or neutral. Being patient with yourself and accepting how this exercise is for you today.

Phase 2: Setting the intention now to notice whatever arises in the attentional field, expanding awareness to curiously notice anything that makes itself known. Breathing sensations, other body sensations, sounds, smells, thoughts, emotions, or something else. Notice things happening inside you and around you in the surroundings. Open your eyes to also take in the sense of sight if this feels comfortable.

Allow these various observations to be just as they are, as they arise and fade away from your awareness. Be patient with yourself as you bring mindful awareness to everything you notice. This is a new way of being aware of your present-moment experiences.

With the next exhale, release this exercise, opening your eyes if they are closed and focusing on something else.

Modifications

Try this exercise in different situations, in your day-to-day life.

Shreyasi and Frank Brodhecker

Exercise #12: Other ways to be mindful around your horse

(Loosely adapted from Handout 4A, Linehan, 2015b)

Fiona and Honey, SJ Originals Photography

Intro

We offer here a list of opportunities to briefly practise mindful awareness through the day, both at and away from the barn. Now that you have a sense of how to practise paying attention mindfully through the other exercises, it is hopefully more natural to notice things in this way.

Context

On your own; at times, across the fence or with your horse

This list offers several ways to immediately tune in to the present moment when you are with your horse. These are ways that you can include brief mindful moments in your day.

1. Watch your horse at a distance as they eat their feed or hay. Notice the visual appearance of things, sounds in the environment, and your horse's movements. Note the chewing rhythm. Notice your horse's emotional state. Notice your own emotional state.

2. When you go out to the pasture to visit or catch a horse that is far away, take a mindful walk towards the horse. Specifically—walk towards your horse mindfully, rather than "mind-full-y."

3. Try walking in a non-straight line in your horse's paddock or pasture. Pay attention to when the horses notice you—each time a horse head comes up, pause, and breathe until the head goes back down.

4. When walking with your horse from one point to another, take a few moments to mindfully notice walking with your horse. As above, walk with your horse mindfully, rather than "mind-full-y."

5. Stand by the fence and watch your horse within the herd. How does your horse interact with the other horses? Does your horse have specific buddies? Does your horse prefer to stand off to the side? How can you tell that your horse is also watching you or is aware in another way?

6. Set the vibrate alarm on your phone to one minute and then mindfully notice just one feature of your horse's body, such as the

right hoof, muzzle, or tail. The reason for setting the vibrate tone is so that your horse isn't spooked when the alarm is activated at the end of the one-minute time period.

7. Listen to the sounds around you as you stand near your horse. Notice the textures and shapes of the sounds around you. Listen to the silence between the sounds.

8. Play some music near your horse. Listen to the music, notice your physical and emotional response, and watch how your horse responds. We recommend classical or instrumental music at first and that you avoid loud jarring sounds (regardless of genre) as they tend to alarm a horse.

9. While standing in the barn, breathe in and notice the smells around you. Bring some hay or tack close to your nose and notice the smell. Take it away and notice whether the smell lingers.

10. Touch something near you. For example, you could touch a surface such as the wall, a fence, or an item of tack. Notice the texture and the sensations on your skin.

11. Pet the barn cat or dog. Notice the feeling of the fur against your hands and the expression in the animal's eyes. Listen to the sound of purring or breathing.

12. Notice your horse's eyes for brief moments, using soft eyes. Pay attention to the colour of your horse's eyes, the expression, and reflections from the surroundings. Notice whether the horse is communicating anything in particular—sense this, rather than thinking about it. Then, blink slowly at your horse and look away.

The next few exercises can be practised on your own or with your horse.

13. Focus your attention on the sensations in your chest. Can you feel anything there? How does it change from one moment to the next?

14. Keeping your focus on what you are currently doing, gently expand your awareness to include the space around you.

15. As you look at an object in front of you, relax your vision and start to notice the periphery with soft eyes.

Sharing the Present

16. Practise adjusting your seat (as you sit at the edge of a chair) so that you are engaging a neutral pelvis.

17. When a feeling arises within you, notice it—perhaps by saying to yourself, "A feeling of sadness is arising within me."

18. When a thought arises within you, notice it—perhaps saying to yourself, "The thought, 'It is hot in here,' is arising within me."

19. Take a few moments to create a mental picture of being with your horse—however that may look—and feel gratitude for the time you spend together.

20. Take a few moments to create a mental picture of you and your horse together, and allow positive, caring, or loving feelings to flow between the two of you.

SUMMARY
Closing reflections

You want to get that horse feeling so good that it would rather spend time with you than do anything else.
~~ Tom Dorrance, *More Than a Horseman*

This project arose from our realization that many opportunities exist for everyday mindfulness with your horse and that incorporating mindful awareness and attitudes into the time you spend together can have a positive impact on your relationship. We have attempted to provide a theoretical description of what it means to be mindful and to notice events in the present moment with attitudes of patience, non-judgment, curiosity, acceptance, compassion, and letting go. We briefly explored some common questions about mindfulness and the personal benefits of mindfulness practice as evidenced in current research. We created these exercises and offered reflections rooted in our own experience with our horses; our aim with this book is that these assist you in your journey to better connect with the horses in your life.

We hope that practising the exercises in this book has given you first-hand experience of what it means to be mindfully aware of your life in each present moment. Mindfulness is not about thinking, but about sensing and feeling. Nothing we say to describe mindfulness with words will ever compare to you living in mindful awareness for brief moments of your day. By starting to practise mindful awareness in the earlier exercises in the book—through paying mindful attention to your senses, your breathing patterns, and then to your physical being—you explored a different way of being around your horse. We hope that noticing thoughts and emotions allowed you to reflect on the degree to which you can feel aware of and able to handle such experiences without being overwhelmed.

Exercises for appreciating your horse, being able to repair the relationship with your horse when things get tough and letting go are higher-level activities to strengthen your observations of the horse-human relationship. Finally, we tried the mindful practice of noticing more than one event in each present moment, in the exercise "Putting it all together." We concluded with shorter exercises to practise in brief time periods, in "Other ways to be mindful around your horse."

Horses are innately mindful, and we hope that trying these exercises with your horse created changes in your communication and with observing and responding to horse behaviours. Ideally, this practice has helped you to understand your horse better than you did before. We also hope that you feel a stronger connection to your horse and have greater appreciation for what horses give you daily.

Mindfulness practice is a lifelong journey, and we invite you to continue with it and notice how practising affects your personal life and your time with your horse. We wish you space and openness to integrate mindful awareness into your time inside and outside of the barn, apart from just practising these exercises. We enthusiastically believe that this journey will have an immense impact on your own emotional well-being and on your horse's emotional well-being. At the end of the day, our hope for you is that you feel closer to your horse.

Sharing the Present

The journey continues, SJ Originals Photography